Participating in architectural competitions:
a guide for competitors, promoters and assessors

Participating in architectural competitions:

A guide for competitors, promoters and assessors

Judith Strong

The Architectural Press Ltd
London

Photographic acknowledgements

The Architects' Journal: la; *Brecht-Einzig Ltd*: 1b, 2a, 10; *Jo Reid/Cason Conder & Partners*: 3b; *John Whybrow Ltd/Burman Goodall & Partners*: 41; *Robert J. Anderson & Co*: 5b; *Courtesy of The Director, Glasgow Art Gallery and Museum*: 8; *Patricia Cain/Casson Conder & Partners*: 9; *Henk Snoek Photography & Associates*: 12; *John Donat Photography*: 13; *Spence & Webster*: 14

First published in 1976 by The Architectural Press Ltd: London

ISBN: 0 85139 514 7
© Judith Strong 1976

The Regulations for the Promotion and Conduct of Competitions and the Regulations for International Competitions in Architecture and Town Planning are reproduced with the permission of RIBA Publications Ltd and the International Union of Architects, the respective copyright holders

Photoset by Red Lion Setters, Holborn, London
Printed in Great Britain by R.J. Acford Ltd, Chichester

Contents

Foreword

If you want to know anything about architectural competitions you will find it in here. This comprehensive handbook is unique: it really is the only book of its kind. Although written mainly for architects, it will provide an invaluable guide to anyone involved or interested in architectural competitions.

I have observed that those countries with high architectural achievements and where architects are in good standing with the public are where architectural competitions are most actively used to select architects. The benefits of these competitions to building promoters, to architects and to the public are considerable, but it is necessarily a complicated topic and needs a better understanding.

Judith Strong has been looking after competitions at the RIBA for some years and she is not only enthusiastic about their role, she understands how they work and what pitfalls to avoid. The range of information is mainly concerned with this country, but there is also some useful guidance on the European situation, the Commonwealth countries and the situation in the USA.

If we want our architecture to flourish, to be relevant to today's needs and to be *enjoyed* by the public, we need a constant flow of architectural competitions. I am sure that this expert book will help that process.

Eric Lyons
President of the Royal
Institute of British
Architects 1975-77

Introduction

This book is written as a handbook on competitions: a source of information and reference for competitors, assessors and promoters on the organisation of competitions and a guide to the thinking which lies behind the competition system. I am not an architect but neither can I claim to be an independent observer, having spent seven years in the Public Affairs Department of the Royal Institute of British Architects, advising on competitions, promoting the system and publicising the results. This book aims to set out facts, supported wherever possible by my own experience and by the experience of numerous other people — architects, other professionals and laymen — who have been involved with competitions. It does not set out to persuade or convert, but where there is a bias, it is in favour of extending the competition system. I make no apology for this because I believe that a more flourishing competition system can only help to improve the quality of design, the morale of the profession and the attitude of the public to what is being built around them. The research I have done for this book and the enthusiasm for the competition system of so many of the people I have talked to have fully reinforced this opinion.

Although there are chapters in this book on the organisation of competitions and the attitudes towards them in Europe, the USA and the Commonwealth, much of the information is based on the UK experience, mainly during the last decade. About ten years ago Eric Lyons finally managed to open up the competition debate within the RIBA and to persuade its Council to launch a long-term project exploring the possibilities of the competition system. This began by a complete revision of the RIBA regulations and supporting documents, which were published in 1968. As a result the RIBA is the one organisation, outside of those countries which have maintained a steady flow of competitions as part of the normal working environment, to have studied the competition system in depth and to have promoted it systematically. Its overt success as yet has not been great, and has certainly not been helped by the prolonged reorganisation of local government or by the subsequent slump in the building industry (I am not suggesting that the two are in any way connected), but attitudes are changing. The competition system is far from dead, either in the UK or elsewhere in the world, and the experience the RIBA has gained will prove valuable to other organisations considering similar projects. Furthermore the versatility which has been introduced into the system in the UK has a relevance wherever competitions are being considered and promoted.

Obviously, working with the RIBA for so long has coloured my thinking, but I would like to stress that the opinions given in this book are most definitely my own (except when placed in quotation marks or specifically attributed to someone else). They do not represent the policy of the RIBA nor are they necessarily the opinions of the Competitions Working Group, though I hope they will be in sympathy with most of what I have written as, without their work over many years, there would have been little point to this book.

I would like to thank all the people who have helped me with the research: the architects who filled in my long questionnaires (they are quoted in the text but not identified personally) and dug out old records to give me an indication of the time they had spent on competitions and the costs involved; the assessors who took the trouble to analyse their experience and explain their motives; the people from other professions involved in competitions, who gave up their time to talk to me; and my colleagues from overseas institutes for letting me have their views and sending information on the organisation of competitions in their countries.

In two thousand, four hundred and twenty-four years of organised architectural competitions, this is, as far as I know, the first reference book on how the system works. Though we have done without it for so long, I hope, now that it is written it will, like the safety pin, prove useful.

Judith Strong
May 1976

2

1 Background to the competition system

A brief history

Architectural competitions have been with us for a very long time. In fact, a competition is recorded as early as 448 BC when the Boule (senate or council) of Athens invited designs from architects for a war memorial on the Acropolis, and even prescribed the scale for the designs. In Renaissance Italy, the architects and craftsmen had to compete for the commissions which were to make their reputation. Brunelleschi's design for the cupola of Florence Cathedral was the result of a competition held in 1418 and was followed soon after by a competition for the famous golden doors of the Baptistry.

In France a competition was held in 1665 for the completion of the Louvre, and early uses of the system in this country produced the Bank of England (1788), the National Gallery (1832) and the Houses of Parliament (1835). In Victorian England, with over a hundred competitions a year, the system produced numerous churches, city halls (Manchester, Cardiff and Glasgow), the Law Courts, St Pancras Hotel, the Victoria and Albert Museum, Liverpool Cathedral (won by Giles Scott at the age of twenty-two) and even Nelson's Column (though top and bottom came from two separate entries). There were so many complaints about the way these were run that the Royal Institute of British Architects set its mind to drawing up the first basic rules for organising competitions. Discussions to bring some fairness into the system had already begun when the RIBA was formed in 1834. Letters continued to be written and heated speeches made and by 1872 a special committee had drawn up regulations asking for qualified assessors, a reasonable prize fund and a commitment to the winner on the part of the promoter. However, it was not until 1907 that these mandatory, by which time the great Victorian competition bonanza was over.

During the first half of the twentieth century the system continued to be used in its new, properly organised form, and about twenty-five competitions were promoted on average each year. London's County Hall, Guildford Cathedral and the RIBA building all belong to competitions of this period. After the Second World War, with the change in the sort of buildings to which public money was being directed and the growth of the design teams within local authority departments, the number of competitions fell to about ten a year. At some stage the RIBA introduced a clause requiring the promoter to pay a prohibitive 1.5% of the project value if the winning architect could not proceed with the job and competitions gradually became a rare event. In 1968, encouraged, possibly, by Parliamentary interest in the Commonwealth competition for the design of the new extension to the Houses of Parliament, and certainly by the dedicated persistence of Eric Lyons, the RIBA had a long look at its regulations and undertook a detailed revision.

Armed with a sound new basic system and the stated support of the RIBA Council, the Competitions Working Group set about the more difficult task of persuading clients to promote competitions. The profession is still by no means wholeheartedly behind this effort but those who support the system (and there are many who do) are firmly convinced that it has a unique and continuing role to play in maintaining vitality and individuality in architecture.

The history of competitions is a fascinating subject, especially for those who enjoy intrigue, but it is not the subject of this book. Anyone who wants to go into more detail should read Frank Jenkins's *Architect and Patron* (Oxford, 1961) or the introduction to the exhibition catalogue *Marble Halls*, by John Physick and Michael Darby (Victoria and Albert Museum, 1973).

Jurisdiction over competitions

In nearly all cases where there is an established organisation of architects, control is exercised over fees and competitive work, and a system devised to allow members to take part in approved architectural competitions.

Under the present RIBA Code of Professional Conduct no member may "compete with another architect by means of a reduction of fees or by means of other inducements" and no one is permitted to "take part in or be associated in any way with the carrying out of a design selected as the result of a competition which does not have RIBA approval". The RIBA has drawn up a document *Regulations for the Promotion and Conduct of Competitions* which must be followed whenever RIBA members are invited as architects, to submit professional design work in competition with one another without the payment of a fee. At an international level, the RIBA accepts the jurisdiction of the International Union of Architects (UIA), which has drawn up regulations for the organisation of competitions among

4

architects from different countries. This means that nearly all competitive work within the United Kingdom is controlled by the RIBA, either directly or through the UIA, and any member who does work on a speculative basis or enters a competition which is not approved by the RIBA or the UIA may find himself in breach of the Code of Professional Conduct.

(See Chapter 5, "Legal and professional aspects of competitions" and Chapter 10, "International competitions".)

Other types of competitive work
RIBA members are permitted to undertake competitive, as distinct from speculative, work provided they are paid fees in accordance with the scale of professional charges sanctioned and published by the RIBA which are appropriate to the work undertaken. (Not all architectural institutes make this distinction. In some cases a situation falls within the jurisdiction of an institute's competition regulations whenever two or more architects are asked to prepare designs simultaneously for the same project.) The RIBA definition means that a client could commission a number of architects to prepare feasibility studies or sketch design schemes without promoting a competition. He would, however, be committed to paying up to 2% of the project value (depending on the stage to which the work was taken) to each architect submitting a sketch design. By comparison, a competition would cost between .5% and 2% of the project value, including the payment of assessors' fees, for an unlimited number of designs.

The RIBA does not have jurisdiction over competitions where the speculative element is borne by a developer rather than an architect (i.e. in the competitive tender and design/build situation). In such cases the architect should be paid the proper fees for the design work he does for his client (i.e. the developer) regardless of whether his team finally carries out the work.

The RIBA Code requires that "members or students asked to take part in a limited competition (i.e. where named architects are specifically invited to submit designs) must at once notify the Secretary of the RIBA, submitting particulars of the competition". In any situation, therefore, where terms other than the normal fee scale (either on a time charge or stage basis) are offered to a member, the RIBA should be informed. It is likely that such an offer either would fall within the jurisdiction of the competition system or if taken up would be regarded as speculative work. This would apply to RIBA members practising within the United Kingdom or elsewhere. Members of other architectural institutes throughout the world are generally bound by similar regulations.

5

Non-architectural competitions

There are a number of competitions in the UK each year which, although of interest to architects, do not necessarily require architectural solutions (for instance, ideas on improving a particular street or open space, sculpture competitions, interior design or planning competitions). Some of these fall within the jurisdiction of other professional organisations and are limited to their own members; others are of a more general nature and will have an open entry. Where RIBA members are also members of other professional institutes (e.g. the Royal Town Planning Institute or the Institute of Landscape Architects) they have a right to enter any competitions run in accordance with the competition rules of these institutes. With a project which requires the skills of several allied professions, the institutes concerned may co-operate to promote a joint competition open to all members. (The River Clyde study and ideas competition, promoted by the Corporation of Glasgow in 1973, was organised in association with the RIBA, the RTPI and the ILA.) In most other countries, architects, planners and landscape architects are not regarded as distinct professions and are members of the one organisation. In certain countries membership might also extend to engineers and interior designers, who would be eligible to enter the competitions in the country concerned and UIA competitions.

For competitions of a more general nature in the UK, the RIBA would provide help and advice on the organisation, if requested, but would not claim any jurisdiction or seek to impose its regulations. The UIA takes a similar view on international competitions of a general nature. (A UK example is the recent series of Art into Landscape competitions, promoted by the Arts Council, for ideas for brightening up odd areas of left-over space. The RIBA was consulted and invited to nominate an assessor but did not ask that the regulations for architectural competitions should be followed in every respect.)

If an RIBA member is in doubt as to whether a competition falls within the jurisdiction of the RIBA or whether he is involved in a competition situation which is properly covered by RIBA regulations, he should consult the RIBA Secretariat. Similarly, members of other professional institutes should refer to their appropriate organisations.

6

2 How the system works in the UK

A competition is a means by which a promoter may call upon a number of architects to study a problem and work out solutions. Experience shows that an entirely unco-ordinated competitive situation, in the long term, benefits neither the clients nor the profession. Many of the intrigues and so-called "outrages" of the free competitive situation of the last century belonged to a time when professional ethics were generally less scrupulous than they are today. An organised system of competition, in which architects have confidence, attracts a higher standard of entry and appeals to the more committed sections of the profession, which must be to the promoters' advantage. The current RIBA regulations provide for two basic types of competition: project competitions and ideas competitions; and the aim of the system underlying them is to organise competitive work so that the architects are ensured of a fair deal and the promoter is given the best answer to his stated requirements. Whether the present system achieves this in every respect or attempts to over-protect one side at the expense of another are matters for debate, but few people would question the necessity of a properly organised system. Opponents of competitions question the whole idea of unpaid architectural design work, not whether it should be controlled or left open.

Project competitions
Project competitions are used where the promoter wants a design for a project he intends to build. Architects are invited to submit designs in accordance with the specific brief which sets out the requirements of the promoter in detail. These competitions may be open to all registered architects or limited by invitation or region. They may also be organised in one or two stages, but where there is an intention to build there must also be a commitment to the winning architect by the promoter and this is written into the conditions.

Ideas competitions
Ideas competitions, on the other hand, are used to explore situations,

7

to search for alternative solutions to existing problems and to stimulate the discussion of new ideas. The brief is broadly based so that all aspects of the subject may be studied. This more general approach is reflected in the prize fund, which may offer equal prizes to alternative solutions rather than an outright award to the single best scheme. In any case the ideas competition commits the promoter to nothing other than to pay the prizes offered, in accordance with the assessors' award.

Ideas leading to a project
There are occasions when neither a straight ideas competition nor a project competition is appropriate and modifications of these basic types exist within the system.

When a long-term plan is required or the promoter is not directly responsible for implementing a design, a competition may contain a clause offering to appoint the winning architect as consultant if any major part of his design is to be implemented or to negotiate terms. Moving more closely to the project competition the RIBA has recently introduced a hybrid called the Preliminary Project Competition. This is designed to help the promoter who intends to build but wants to look at possible methods of tackling the problem before establishing a detailed brief. The competition aims, not to provide an approved design, but to find an architect with the right approach to the subject; the promoter is not committed to appoint the winning architect for the whole scheme but is bound to commission him to undertake further studies.

A variant of this approach was used successfully in the Ashton Court competition promoted by Bristol Corporation, where the problem was one of adapting and extending a historic house. Assessors were appointed and architects were invited to submit details of their approach to and experience of this type of work. A shortlist of architects was drawn up and they were invited to take part in a limited competition.

Developer/Architect competitions
The Developer/Architect competition is a specific type of project competition which was introduced to provide an alternative to competitive tender, where developers submit a design for an area, together with an offer price for the land or contract to build. The RIBA felt it was necessary to separate the financial considerations from those of design and community needs and so the principle of the Developer/Architect competition was established: that the financial

agreement must be agreed at the outset and stated in the conditions. This type of competition has been used so far only by New Town authorities for housing projects but it was set up with central area development in mind.

Regional Special Category competitions
In 1974, in response to an initiative by the Glasgow Institute of Architects, a special type of competition was introduced which was designed to encourage local authorities to promote competitions by providing them with a system which cost no more and took no longer than commissioning a private architect in the normal way. The system depends on the RIBA regions setting up committees (comprising four or five architects from private practice, local authorities and architectural schools) to organise the competitions. Local practices are invited to apply for consideration and submit details of their work, and about six practices are selected to take part in each competition. As in all competitions, assessors are appointed to advise the promoter and select the winning design but in this case they do not require a fee. The normal question and answer period is replaced by a "forum" at which the competitors, the promoter and the assessors meet to discuss the brief and clarify the promoter's requirements. The designs are then developed in outline and the winner is selected by the assessors. There are no prizes but there is an undertaking that the winner will be appointed as architect for the work. The whole competition can be run in less than three months as against the ten to fifteen months required for a normal competition. At the time this book went to press, the Regional Special Category competition was being run on an experimental basis by special approval of the President of the RIBA and was limited to local authorities and charitable organisations. However, where used, these competitions were successful so it is likely that the regulations will be amended to incorporate them into the system.

Promoter Choice competitions
While Regional Special Category competitions were introduced as an alternative for the promoter who felt that the time scale for the normal competition was too extended and the additional cost was difficult to budget for, the Promoter Choice competition was brought in to help the promoter who felt unwilling to commit himself to one selected design, even though he was represented on the jury of assessors.
    The Promoter Choice competition differs very little from the standard single-stage project competition except that the jury (it is

recommended that it be made up entirely of architects and, where appropriate, members of allied professions) selects the three or four best designs submitted and the promoter then chooses the one he wishes to build. He does not have to make this choice until he has had a chance to interview the architects responsible for the selected schemes. The chairman of the assessors is also available to help and advise on the final selection.

This type of competition was introduced on an experimental basis in February 1975 and at the time of writing has not yet been used. If the RIBA Council does decide to retain it as part of the standard alternative to the existing types of competitions, it will bring the RIBA system far closer to those organised in Europe.

Although the preceding paragraphs cover the main types of competitions they are not exhaustive. Within the regulations, the system is designed to be flexible and a competition may be a combination of more than one type or it may be specially designed to meet the requirements of one specific situation.

Basic principles
The general principles are the same for all competitions and are universal: that all competitors enter on an equal basis, that anonymity be observed throughout and that the assessment be made on merit alone.

In any RIBA competition, the conditions — which include the rules by which the competition is to be run, the brief, background information, maps and plans and instructions on the submission of designs — are issued to all competitors, who are then given a set time in which to study the conditions and ask questions to elucidate the brief. A document based on these questions is circulated to all competitors, who then have a further set period in which to work on the design. The designs are submitted in accordance with the instructions set out in the conditions and are accompanied by a sealed envelope containing the name of the competitor. The assessors study the designs submitted, make their award and report to the promoter. Only then are the sealed envelopes opened and the names of the competitors known.

In a two-stage competition the first stage is open to any architect who wishes to compete (provided he is eligible). Six or ten of the most promising designs are selected and the authors of these designs are asked to develop them in more detail before the assessors make their final decision. In this case the promoter informs the second-stage competitors, who are known to him but remain as numbers to the assessors until the final decision is made.

The most important single factor in any competition is the quality of the assessors, as they are responsible for the whole conduct of the competition. According to the RIBA regulations they should be appointed right at the outset of the competition because their first job is to ascertain the requirements of the promoter and incorporate these into the competition conditions. The RIBA regulations require that independent architects, nominated by the President of the RIBA, form the majority of the jury, although the promoter is encouraged to be represented. It is the job of the assessors to find, through the competition, a design which gives the best solution within the terms of the brief and to report their decision to the promoter. (See Chapter 9, "The work of the assessors".)

Documentation

The document *Regulations for the Promotion and Conduct of Competitions* (revised 1968) and a paper setting out subsequent amendments are printed in the appendices to this book. The RIBA papers giving guidance on the cost and time required for the main categories of competitions and outlining the basic principles of the Deverloper/Architect, Preliminary Project, Promoter Choice and Regional Special Category competitions can be obtained from the RIBA Competitions Office.

3 Entering competitions: working methods, cost and time

Who enters and why?
Traditionally, competitions have attracted young architects who see them as an opportunity to make their names and set up in practice, but, although their role is important in discovering new talent and helping to establish young practices, their appeal is a much wider one.

Ideas competitions get the vast majority of entries from students, who are not able to enter project competitions except in association with a registered architect, and recently qualified architects, although some older members see these competitions as a chance to design something outside the usual routine and will work on an entry in their spare time. With project competitions, however, entries come from a wide cross-section of the profession — from the individual architect, working at home in the evenings and weekends, to the large, established practice, carrying the job as part of the normal office situation. The second-stage competitors of recent large UK project competitions (the Burrell Museum, the Northampton County Hall and the New Parliamentary Building competitions) reflect this cross-section of interest quite markedly. In each case the six or so second-stage competitors included teams of young architects, employed in public or private offices or in teaching; practices beginning to establish themselves; and well-known names. With so few competitions, it is unwise to draw conclusions from the results, but it is interesting to note that in each case the competition was won by the young group of individuals, with a well-established practice falling in second place.

A lot of practices never enter competitions — some as a matter of principle, others because their type of practice is based on the sort of work which does not go out to competition (for instance, firms dealing mainly with commercial developers or small practices with strong local links though the latter are being drawn into locally organised competitions). But there are few architects who have never entered any sort of competition, and once a feeling for competition work has been established it often seems to stick. Many partners in private practice look to the competition system to provide opportunities for research, to invigorate and stimulate the office during the routine job, to keep in touch with current design thinking and to provide an opportunity to design rather than administer. Most people say they enter competitions in order to win them and get the commission for the project, and it is true that this is one of the few ways, within the RIBA Code of Professional Conduct, that an architect can draw the attention of a possible client to the quality of his work. This means that competitions are used both by young practices to get new work and by more established practices to try to extend the range of work they do, or to introduce new clients. One of the attractions of a competition such as that promoted by the Greater London Council for housing at Royal Mint Square was that the promoters would also be commissioning architects for future projects and might well consider some of the competitors whose schemes they liked. The competition attracted almost 300 designs.

But architects know that they are up against some of the most talented and enthusiastic members of the profession when they enter a competition and that there will be several good schemes which do not win. In the present situation, therefore, any architect who enters a competition solely to get the job will soon become disillusioned. That architects continue to enter competitions in such large numbers indicates that there must be other reasons than the outside chance of winning. In order to explore different approaches to design solutions, architects need real projects and practical briefs and competitions provide these. The main motivation is probably the belief that there are better solutions to current design problems than those generally being offered and that they must be discussed and considered. Ideas with potential need to be shown to work if they are to have any impact, but unfortunately, with so few competitions and so many entries, much of this valuable research element is being lost.

Working on the design
One of the great differences between working on a project in the normal way and designing in response to a competition brief is that in the preliminary stages of competition design the architect and the client do not meet. This affects the way the job is tackled in that the designer must be both the protagonist for the scheme and its main critic. The architect cannot try out an idea on a client to see how he reacts before incorporating it in the design and developing it in detail but must anticipate reactions, take decisions and then justify his own approach. For this reason many competitors try to build a system of interaction and criticism into the design team.

14

An architect in a practice which was established and still gets work through the competition system described the way his office sets about developing a competition entry as follows:

"The principle is that the partners design the building in committee and that the 'office' only comes into it to provide
   i) a junior who acts as a sort of graphic 'secretary' (see what it looks like if drawn accurately!)
   ii) mass help with 'drawing out', although the final drawing is sometimes done by the partners.

"All the partners and the 'secretary' visit the site, preferably together. They take a lot of photographs to cover the atmosphere of a large surrounding area.

"The 'secretary' produces several copies of a 'design kit', one for each partner, and this is made up of the conditions, graphic representation of the accommodation to the same scale as the reduced site plan, photos, and certain analytical diagrams.

"The partners then have a conceptual competition amongst themselves working in private, for about two weeks, and this is followed by a series of evening meetings at which each puts forward his ideas in a room wallpapered with plain paper, on which they draw as they talk; lots of subjective talk. Sometimes the different ideas quickly draw together, on another occasion two different concepts developed from the ideas of two partners were left on the table. In this case, the two partners then had a friendly competition (but still very diagrammatic), to prove their ideas to a stage further till it was agreed without dispute which basic concept was right. By then the two previously opposing partners knew more than the others and became joint partners in charge. The meetings with all the partners still continued but, by now, over drawing boards. In other schemes there was no partner or partners in charge as no one ever knew each other very well. Some schemes have been developed right through to detail and drawn out by the partners, in other cases one or two partners and the graphic secretary (joined towards the end by two other assistants) developed the design. It was then traced by others while the partners went on holiday."

The system described here of alternating periods of individual thinking with group sessions to develop ideas and then refine them through discussion and criticism is one that works well for competition projects, whether the group is a practice or a number of architects who have got together for the one project.

This group empathy can, however, be difficult to achieve and some architects feel that the best ideas emerge from less of a compromise situation, with an individual working alone or calling in help only on research and drawing out.

"I have found after entering eight competitions in my career that the best ideas usually come out of the individual or the individual-dominated team. Ideally I feel that a real team effort would result in a better building, but only in two of the eight instances have I found someone close enough that a real, shared design experience was possible."

Even where an individual is working alone on a strongly motivated personal solution, a "blasting session" with colleagues can be helpful, if only to force the designer to define his standpoint and clarify his position. It is this sort of scrutiny which a scheme will finally have to stand up to if it is to have any chance of winning, because when the assessors are pulling the scheme apart the designer will not be there to explain and defend it. If there are weaknesses or concepts which do not stand up to criticism, brainstorming sessions at various stages in the development of the scheme will help to identify them.

When a practice enters a competition it is rarely treated as a normal job. One or two partners will work on a scheme which interests them, often in their spare time, drawing on help from the practice only when peaks build up. In other cases where the partners decide that it would benefit a practice to submit an entry, there could be a "preliminary competition" within the office and the individual whose scheme is selected as the basis of the office submission works on it, meeting the partners to discuss and develop the scheme as it goes on.

In countries where competitions are one of the everyday ways of gaining a commission (such as Germany or Switzerland), a practice may take on staff who are specifically chosen for competition work and devote a high proportion of their time to preparing entries. Few architects in the UK have the opportunities to develop such a professional attitude towards competitions and few practices could afford to recruit staff on this basis. It is interesting to note that the team which has the most successful record in UK competitions recently (Ellis and Clayton, who have won five major prizes) includes one partner who spent some time working in Switzerland and entering competitions there.

16

Interpreting the conditions

The conditions for a competition are made up of three basic sections: the general conditions, the instructions to competitors and the brief.

The general conditions spell out the details of the timetable, the prize money, the commitment to the winning architect, etc. The instructions to competitors state what is to be submitted and how it is to be presented. The brief sets out the promoter's requirements, giving background information on the project, details of the site and surrounding area, planning restrictions, accommodation required, cost limits and any other information assessors feel competitors will need in order to prepare a scheme.

Conditions do not normally spell out requirements which are statutory, though they may make reference to the appropriate publication. For instance, in a competition for local authority housing, competitors would be expected to know the current regulations regarding space standards, density, cost yardsticks etc. Where the authority concerned have requirements additional to the national standard, these should be given.

It is the job of the assessors to take the promoter's brief and to put it in a form which is appropriate for the competition. Assessors are asked to keep mandatory requirements to the minimum and give the information the competitors need in such a way as to leave design options as open as possible. Where requirements are mandatory, assessors are directed to make this clear in the conditions. To put this in its simplest form, where the word "must" is used, it indicates that ignoring the requirement would lead to the disqualification of the entry. The words "should" and "may" are not mandatory and denote lesser degrees of necessity.

In the paper *Organising a Competition*, the RIBA gives the following advice to assessors:

> "*Mandatory requirements should be kept to a minimum but where failure to satisfy the brief on a particular point would disqualify an entry this must be stated clearly in the Conditions*".

If such information is not clear, then it is up to the competitor to ask that it be clarified in the explanatory memorandum which is circulated to all competitors at the end of the questions period.

Competitors often try to interpret the brief to find out what design approach is required. For instance, in a recent housing competition the assessors stated that "the entrances to blocks should be treated humanely", which led one competitor to ask whether this indicated that the assessors would not consider any scheme which did not put the housing units in a block form. In fact, no indication was given anywhere else in the conditions as to the form the development should take apart from a general height restriction. The statement was intended to indicate how entrances to several dwellings, if the scheme was designed in this way, should be treated. Competition conditions are not written as the basis of a game of "hunt the thimble" but to give as much information as possible to competitors without imposing a design solution.

Statements in the conditions are best read in their context and accepted at their face value, for though assessors may occasionally appear devious, their intention is to help the competitor, not to mislead him. Competitors tend to feel that assessors should indicate in the conditions the sort of solution they are looking for, a view encouraged by the fact that assessors in past competitions have sometimes selected schemes all following the same approach. But if the promoter knows exactly what he wants, he is not likely to hold a competition. If, having studied all the schemes submitted, the assessors come to the conclusion that a certain approach has invariably led to a better solution to the problem, then the competition has proved the point. What is self-evident at the end of a competition is not necessarily so when the conditions are being drawn up.

In the RIBA competition system, entries are supposed to abide by the conditions and answer the brief. Assessors are appointed early in the process, and having had a chance to influence the brief and been responsible for drawing up the conditions, they are expected to abide by them and make an assessment based on the stated requirements. If, as people sometimes claim, a scheme is selected which does not fulfil all the requirements of the brief as set out in the conditions, it may be because the assessors have decided, in good faith, that the solution was within an acceptable margin of the stated requirements and could be regarded as a bona fide entry and that its merits justified its selection. To define this margin of tolerance is extremely difficult and it depends to a certain extent on the quality of the other schemes submitted. In principle, no such margin exists, but in practice it does seem that a good scheme which answers most of the requirements, may beat a mediocre scheme which fulfils the demands of a check list of factual criteria. But a good scheme which answers the brief in every respect will beat them both.

Where there are a very few competitions attracting a large number of entries, competitors can be tempted to go for "impact", fearing that a quiet scheme, however well worked out and sensitively detailed, will not attract the assessors' attention. Though understandable in the present situation, the idea that a competition winner must be a striking building rather than a building of high quality is not really valid and, in the long term, is detrimental to the competition system.

The mandatory requirements, should, therefore, be taken as absolute. If a competitor chooses to ignore the conditions, he may prove his own particular point and get good publicity for his design, but he risks being disqualified from the competition.

(The roles and attitudes of assessors are discussed in more detail in Chapter 9.)

Asking questions
Some ideas competitions and most project competitions give competitors the opportunity to ask questions. Once the conditions have been issued to competitors a period of about six to eight weeks is allowed for submitting questions. The purpose of the question period is to allow competitors to study the brief and seek any additional information they may require. It also acts as a useful check for the assessors.

When the RIBA regulations were last revised, the old system where every question was set out with an appropriate answer was abandoned in favour of a more flexible approach. Assessors are now directed to issue an explanatory document based on the questions received, giving competitors any further information which the questions indicate is required. In some recent competitions the old system has continued in use but this will happen less frequently as the revised approach becomes more established.

An alternative to the written question and answer system is a meeting to which competitors, promoters and assessors are invited to discuss the brief. This system had already been introduced in Regional Special Category competitions and in limited competitions in the UK and has been used successfully in other countries. (See Chapter 9.)

Visiting the site
Competitions have been won by architects who did not visit the site and except for limited or Regional Special Category competitions, the conditions are drawn up on the assumption that not all competitors will be able to make the journey. However, most competitors do try to visit the site, and the promoter will expect to make arrangements where the site is not readily accessible to the public. Details of these will be given in the conditions.

Time: design time and competition timetables
Ideas, single-stage and two-stage competitions take about six, ten and fifteen months respectively from the launching of the competition to the announcement of the results. Most competitions allow three months' design time at each stage. Where a period for questions is allowed it is additional to this design time which means that competitors have about five months from the launching of the competition to the submission of first-stage designs. Most serious competitors (serious, here, meaning those who have been "placed" in competitions during the last ten years) claim to use nearly all this time for working on an entry, although not on a full-time basis during the first few months.

The design period can be divided up into three main sections, with half the time given to sketching out and discussing possible solutions, 40% to developing the design and 10% to drawing up the submission. It is tempting to leave the design fluid for as long as possible but if an entry is to be properly worked out, with the necessary supporting information to show that it can be built and built within the cost limits given, it is important to decide upon the main principles early in the design period. On average, fewer than 10% of competitors ask questions but of the architects interviewed who had won first, second or third prizes in recent competitions, 50% said that they had submitted questions. This does not necessarily mean that the information they received played a significant part in shaping their winning entries, but it does indicate that they had studied the brief and developed preliminary schemes early on in the competition and this gave them three full months' design time to work on their entries. It is important to leave enough time to think about the presentation of the scheme, from the point of view of what is to be included as well as how it is to be shown.

What does the competition timetable mean in terms of man-hours? The amount of time competitors estimated they spent on a design varied considerably but this may have depended on how they defined "time" (i.e. is thinking in the bath included?). Some practices spend well over 1,000 hours on the two stages of a competition entry, while individuals may win the same competition with much less time input (although it will probably have involved them in working flat out, evenings and weekends, for several months).

To give some examples, in a Developer/Architect competition, one architect estimated the time his practice spent as 320 hours, but another firm, working on a very similar competition organised at the same time, thought they had spent 670 hours on the project. The lowest estimate of time for the first stage of the New Parliamentary Building was 160 hours (this competitor did not make the second stage), whereas one of the prizewinners estimated that the time spent in the first stage was nearer 500 hours. The winner of a limited competition for a prestige civic project estimated that his practice had spent 1,576 hours (610 hours of partners' time and 966 of the junior staff time) on the design and one of the second-stage competitors in the Northampton competition claimed that his practice had spent 1,862 hours on the two stages of the competition. It is more difficult to get the figures for the time that individuals or groups of people not in practice together spend on competitions, as they do not keep a record, but "ages" covers what most people feel about the amount of time required.

Nearly all the figures quoted above came from architects who had been "placed" in the competition they entered, so it can be assumed that the amount of time they spent was sufficient to develop the design to the standard required.

It is unlikely that any individuals or small groups in full-time employment would be able to complete the second stage of a competition without taking some leave (500 hours was one of the lowest estimates of the amount of time required in the second stage).

Costs

If a competition is systematically costed in the same way as a normal job, then the costs of submission are enormous. A large international competition run in two stages could cost a practice as much as £50,000 and a medium-sized project could not be tackled for much under £2,000 even if the design did not reach the second stage. Looked at in this way it is surprising that practices enter competitions, but, although they are aware of the cost in man-hours, architects, both as individuals and as partners in practice, do seem prepared to treat competitions as an extra activity to which they dedicate much of their spare time. Even if an architect is prepared to set aside the cost of labour involved in preparing a competition entry (and he can only do so with any economic justification if the labour is his own), entering competitions can still be an expensive business. The prizes offered, especially in a large two-stage competition, look attractive to the general public but unless a practice wins the competition and gets the job, it has little chance of breaking even. For instance, in a limited competition where the first prize was £2,550 and each honorarium £500, the winning team estimated that their entry, taking into account hours spent, cost the practice over £5,500. In the Northampton

21

County Hall competition one of the second-stage competitors estimated that the cost to his practice had been £8,750; the honorarium was £1,000 and the first prize £7,000.

An individual is in a slightly better position in that he is probably working more or less exclusively in his spare time and does not have to take office overheads into account. But even so, the standard honorarium given to every competitor in the second stage of the competition will do little more than cover out-of-pocket expenses. Site visits for a number of people, specialist fees, costs of block models, working photographs of the site and the preparation of drawings and reports can soon add up to the £500 to £1,000 honorarium that the average two-stage competition offers.

If the figures for a competition are analysed on a comparative basis with the RIBA fee scale, it becomes obvious that the only competitor who ends up in an economically viable position is the winner. A competition costs the promoter, in prizes, honoraria and assessors' fees, an amount equivalent to between .5% and 2% of the value of the project (proportionally less for a larger project), whereas the normal fee for preparing a single design to a similar stage of development (work stages C/D in the RIBA scale of charges) is between 1 and 2%. Even though some of the work which an architect would normally undertake, such as ascertaining the client's requirements, will be done by the competition's assessors, the honoraria given to architects cannot possibly amount to anything like normal fees.

As architects are still prepared to enter competitions in spite of these considerations, it is unlikely that the prize structure will be altered in favour of the architect in the near future.

As far as the financial aspects are concerned, the average competitor does much better in ideas competitions. Here the submissions are often limited to about two A1 or A2 panels and ideas do not have to be presented in such detail, or with so much supporting evidence, as projects. Where such competitions are promoted by a commercial organisation the prizes can be generous. Even in today's terms, £1,000 to £2,000 is quite a reasonable reward for the amount of time the winner spends on many of these competitions, and there is slightly more chance of winning, as fewer people enter ideas competitions than project competitions. However, it has to be admitted that the odds are still very much against making a profit.

(Information on the tax situation is given in Chapter 5, "Legal and professional aspects of competitions".)

4 Submission and presentation of entries

Material to be submitted
The material required for a competition entry is strictly defined and limited and presentation techniques are deliberately kept simple.

The RIBA regulations set the requirements out as follows:

> *"The number, scale and method of finishing the required drawings must be distinctly set forth. The drawings must not be more in number or to a larger scale than necessary clearly to explain the design, and such drawings should be uniform in size, number, scale and mode of presentation. The drawings must be accompanied by a concise typewritten report describing the buildings, explaining their construction, finish and the materials proposed to be used, and giving such information as cannot clearly be shown on the drawings ... In a two-stage competition, the drawings submitted in the first stage should be the minimum required to indicate the principles of the competitor's objectives.*
>
> *"In appropriate circumstances the assessor/s may permit or require the submission (specifically limited in scope) of:*
>
> *a perspective drawings or axonometric drawings in line form (or similar diagrams to indicate three dimensional organisation of a design), or*
>
> *b block models, or photographs of block models, where appropriate, or*
>
> *c explanatory diagrams in competitors' reports.*
>
> *"For two-stage competitions this material should be restricted to the second stage. In all cases the preparation of elaborate drawings or presentation material is to be avoided".* (Regulation 22)

Two-stage competitions
Competitions for large or complex projects are organised in two stages so that the assessors can select the designs they feel show potential in their approach to the problem, and the authors of the six or seven designs selected develop their ideas in more detail for the final selection at the end of the second stage. However, most competitors

give far too much detail in the first stage and assessors have expressed disappointment in the lack of development of many second-stage schemes. They feel that many architects do not take full advantage of the additional time the second stage gives to refine, clarify and substantiate their schemes. The important thing in the first stage is to get across the main principles of the design as simply as possible. At present, when competitions are attracting between 200 and 300 entries, assessors want a clear explanation (whether graphic or written) of how the scheme works and of what led the architect to his particular form of solution and will not want to have to work this out for themselves from the detailed drawings. With so much at stake, competitors obviously want to present a scheme as fully as possible and will do so as long as it is within the terms of the conditions. This may well lead assessors to limit the scope of the presentation still further in the first stage, possibly requiring an illustrated report (of a stated number of pages) rather than detailed plans, elevations and sections.

In the second stage of a competition, the assessors require drawings to a larger scale with enough detail to show whether the scheme fulfils the conditions in all respects, whether it can be built within the cost limits if these are given, what materials and finishes are used in the construction and an indication of the architectural quality of the completed building. Competitors are also asked to submit reports explaining and substantiating the drawings.

In project competitions the promoter is usually committed to appointing the architect responsible for the winning design, as selected by the assessors. The second-stage entry must, therefore, be self-explanatory and enough information must be given for the assessors to reach an informed decision on all aspects of the design such as structural viability, cost, safety, etc. At this stage, their responsibility to the promoter will not allow them to give any competitor the benefit of the doubt as far as the feasibility or cost of a scheme is concerned.

The conditions for every competition set out details concerning material required in the section "Instructions to Competitors" and give exact information on the number, size and scale of the drawings, number of pages in the report, etc. As with all sections of the conditions, strict observance is a legal requirement and presenting an entry in a form other than that specified can lead to disqualification.

Submitting designs

For the convenience of the assessors, most conditions require that the drawings are submitted flat and either are of a substantial material or are mounted on thin card. (Two millimeters can be taken as a definition of "thin".) Assessors do not require the original drawings to be submitted, especially as the standard RIBA conditions require that competitors retain copies of all the designs they submit. Normally, any type of dyeline or photographically reproduced print is acceptable. (See section "Presentation techniques" below.)

The submission of designs is organised to retain anonymity. Competitors are issued with an entry form and an official envelope with the conditions. An official label is often but not invariably included. The entry form has to be completed (see the section in Chapter 5 on forming associations), signed and sealed in the official envelope. The drawings with the report and the sealed envelope have then to be packed and sent or delivered to the promoter or his agent (as stated on the entry form). No receipts are given, as to be valid they would have to identify the package and the person who delivered it, which would contravene the anonymity requirement. The package is opened by a member of the promoting organisation who has no connection with the assessors, and a number is placed on each part of the entry and on the official envelope. The envelopes are stored separately and only opened after the assessors have reached a decision and reported it to the promoter.

Some variations on this standard procedure occur, though the principle of anonymity is maintained. For instance, some international competitions require competitors to mark their entries with a logo or code, which is used to identify the sealed envelope containing the entry form with the name of the competitor. In other systems, the entry is double-wrapped, with the internal wrapping bearing no mark whatsoever. This system is usually employed where the postal authorities require a name of sender on the package.

Duplicate entries

If an individual or team is submitting more than one entry (this is usually permitted but it is advisable to check the conditions and entry form), each entry should be packed separately and the competitors should obtain a duplicate entry form and official envelope from the promoter, preferably well before the closing date. No separate registration fee is payable unless this is specifically stated in the conditions, provided both entries come from the same team. Where one member of the team is working with a number of different groups (for instance, a tutor may enter several schemes from his students in his name in a competition open only to registered architects), the entries are regarded as separate entries, and each team should be distinctly registered.

Deadlines

Competitions must be scrupulously conducted and this means that deadlines are important. Most promoters give a time as well as a date for receipt of entries and a delay of five minutes can result in the disqualification of a scheme. Officially, once the deadline has been reached the competition is closed and promoters are instructed to place on one side all entries which arrive after the given time, whether they are delivered by hand, post or special carrier, and to make a note of the time of arrival and reason given for the delay. The assessors have the right to include late schemes at their discretion but competitors would be extremely unwise to rely on their good nature in this respect.

The number of unavoidable accidents which occur during the final day for submissions is well known and gets to be a joke with promoters as they have to supply last-minute competitors with wrapping paper, and the risks which architects are prepared to take with several months' work are incredible. To give a typical example, in a recent competition there were thirty entries the day before it closed; the number had risen to seventy one hour before the deadline, and there were 119 at the final count. This meant that over a third of the competitors were prepared to risk a minor mishap making all their work useless. It is tempting to state that the winning schemes invariably come from well-organised architects who get their entries in well in time but it is not true. Some winning schemes have been delivered at the last minute and established firms have been known to fail to get entries in on time.

In RIBA competitions the only date given is the closing one for receipt of entries, but some other competition systems require two dates to be given: one, the final date by which entries have to be posted, and the other, the last date for receipt. This system is usually used in international competitions to protect the promoter from arguments over the late arrival of overseas mail.

Delivery services

A few points to note are:

The British Post Office do not accept packages larger than 6ft (1828mm) length, breadth and girth combined (i.e. measure the length and add on the longest circumference measurement across the length), with no one dimension longer than 3ft 6in (1066mm). Securicor do a good quick delivery service, the maximum size being 8 cubic ft (0.23m³), with no one dimension longer than 5 ft (1524mm).

If delivering by hand, check the address in advance; and with a large organisation check the department to which it should go and do not assume that it is always the headquarters building.

There are a number of rail delivery services depending upon which route and depots are being used. Not all of them provide a delivery service from the station of arrival to the promoter.

If sending an entry by post make sure the postmark is clearly stamped. The assessors will then be able to establish whether any delay was due to the delivery service or the lateness of posting.

Presentation techniques
Assessors of past competitions say that what they look for in any entry is the extent to which it fulfils the brief, giving the client the building he has asked for and at a cost which is within the stated limits. They require a clear, precise presentation which explains the concept of the design as economically as possible. However, some architects who have been successful to the extent that they have been "placed" in several competitions do think that, although presentation will not win a competition if the quality of thought is not there in the design, extra care and style in the way the entry is submitted can draw it out of the general mass of entries and ensure that what merit a scheme has will be given every consideration. Putting themselves in the position of an assessor, with several hundred entries to consider, they figure that a scheme which gets across the main idea in a straightforward way stands a good chance of being picked out for more detailed consideration, and good presentation techniques can do a lot to help comprehension. Clear graphics are not difficult to obtain with the various commercial lettering techniques which are available and an assessor, faced with his one-hundredth design, is far more likely to study something he can readily read than to squint at a mass of minute grey handwriting to see if somewhere a really good idea is hidden.

Competitions at the moment tend to limit presentation techniques quite considerably but this may change. Already, much more freedom is being allowed in the presentation of entries for ideas competitions, and international competitions usually require a far greater range of illustrative material than RIBA competitions. The reasons for limiting presentation are basically twofold: one, to make sure that the designs are judged on an equal basis and that it is one of architectural merit, not graphic ability; secondly, to prevent any unfair advantage a practice with large resources would have over a young group or an

27

individual architect. But the RIBA Competitions Group is beginning to feel that such tight restriction of technique (as opposed to the very necessary restriction of the amount to be submitted) is no longer valid. They think that architects qualified to judge competitions are capable of distinguishing a good design from a mere skilful presentation and that far from obscuring the qualities of a design, good presentation can help to clarify them. The validity of the case for protecting young architects is also being questioned, as they often have greater skill with modern presentation techniques than the partners of a long-established practice, educated in different methods. Students certainly have access to facilities which you would not normally find in an architect's office.

The following paragraphs give an indication of the sort of techniques which can be used for competition entries. Not all these are permissible in RIBA project competitions, which are still limited in the main to black and white line drawings, but there are situations where tone, limited colour and full colour techniques can be used.

Black and white line drawings only, no tone, no shadows
"Black and white" means no use of colour allowed, and no tones. It does not exclude dyeline processes which may have a greyish tone, nor would it normally exclude sepia dyeline prints. Normally black and white line presentation includes such techniques as offset litho reproduction and photographic reproduction. Photographic reproduction gives a much deeper tone to the black in line work and is effective where an area of black is needed. The system of TTS (true to scale or velograph) reproduction, which can also be used, gives an appearance of original graphics, but it is difficult to find a printer who still undertakes this work.

Where permitted, tones can be achieved by commercial applications such as letratone, either applied to the original work before copying or applied to the dyeline print. An original which included a second colour could be reproduced in black and white to give an effect of tone.

Where the number of panels to be submitted is limited, the cost of using photographic reproduction rather than dyeline is not exorbitant, especially if it is compared with the cost of the man-hours of work which go into a competition design. Ten pounds would cover the cost of photographic reproduction for a normal competition entry, including the cost of mounting and glazing the finished work.

Limited colour techniques

If a competition allows colour to clarify plans and layout, the simplest method is probably to apply commercial colour films to the black and white dyeline or print where there are large areas to be coloured. With small areas, a dyeline print coloured in with coloured inks (fibre-tipped pens are suitable) can look effective, especially if the panel is mounted on thin board and glazed. Glazing is not expensive and most commercial lettering systems are heat resistant and so can be dry mounted and glazed without damage, but they should not be sprayed as this can destroy the heat-resistant qualities.

An overlay of thin film is not recommended. It is difficult to handle when assessors are considering and discarding a number of schemes and can tear and curl up with wear.

If the competition conditions allow, simple blueprint reproductions can give a clear presentation and both these and photographic prints can be reversed to good effect, giving a white line and lettering on a black or blue ground. Two-colour presentation can also be achieved by printing a colour, with TTS or offset litho, and using black line and lettering over the print. Where a large number of copies are required, offset litho techniques can be used to print several colours but the artwork for this is time-consuming and the cost prohibitive unless a large number of prints are being run off (i.e. it begins to be economic at 200 copies).

Full colour presentation

Where there is no limitation (i.e. where any two-dimensional technique can be used), the most inexpensive way of getting an effective presentation is by collage. (A large supply of magazines is needed so that illustrations of the right style and scale can be selected.) A combination of coloured-up, photographic prints with collage can be used very effectively to give an impression of a finished building in use. It may be worth having the panel professionally mounted and glazed, using a heat-resistant glue. A collage including high-gloss illustrative material could also bubble if subjected to heat for the glazing process.

Photomontage techniques are good, but need to be skilfully done to be effective. They might be used where it is important to show a building in its environment. For instance, the winning architects for the New Parliamentary Building produced photomontage pictures to show their scheme as it would look against the Houses of Parliament, but they employed a professional architectural photographer and did so to present the winning scheme to the public, not as part of their competition entry.

Models

Few competitions require models. This is fortunate as they can be expensive to produce and difficult to transport. However, some assessors find that a model helps to clarify the organisation of a scheme and get across how the whole thing works more fully than a long explanatory report. Where a model is required, it would be a simple block model to explain the massing and the layout because competitors are never expected, in UK competitions at least, to spend time and money on intricate detail. If a more elaborate model is required to present the scheme to the public, this will be commissioned by the promoter once the winner has been chosen and the production costs will be met by the promoter. (It is worth trying to find out whether the promoter intends to build a model of the winning scheme; promoters have been known to go ahead with a model, on the basis of the drawings, without consulting the architect responsible. It can be unnerving for an architect to turn up at a press conference and to be confronted by a model he has never seen, purporting to illustrate his scheme.)

If models are required, it would almost invariably be either in the second stage of a two-stage competition or in a limited competition. In each case, the competitor would be guaranteed a certain amount of prize money, so he might well decide to go to a professional modelmaker for this part of his entry.

Non-professionals should stick to simple presentation methods. The most important thing is that the model illustrates the layout, scale and concept of the design and that it stays together. Competitors are not given the opportunity to reassemble their models before the assessors see them, and they can be moved many times in between delivery and judging. Simple block models are generally the most satisfactory, with landscaping, if required, shown diagrammatically. For instance, large-headed nails can show trees and will stay there, whereas carefully painted pieces of loofah may come adrift and break a more important bit of the model.

Photographs of models

Some international competitions require photographs of models instead of, or sometimes as well as, the models themselves. Overall photographs of models can help to show the plan and layout, and well-chosen eye-level shots can also be used to give a feeling of the scale of the building. To take the model of the Parliamentary Building as an example, when it was on display at the RIBA, the architects pasted a thick black band round the sides of the case so that people had to get their eyes down to its street level and look up and into the model building, which gave a very different impression from the God's eye view that the Members of Parliament had given it.

Photographs of models can also be used to give an impression of the completed building in its site. The winners of the Northampton competition actually carried their model of the winning building into a Northamptonshire field to take a distant shot of the reflected clouds and gazing cows, but most competitors used photomontage techniques. Where the shape of the building is important, "sunset" shots of the model — dark (and therefore detailless) against a light sky — can look realistic.

Eric Lyons, in his prize-winning scheme for the Vilamoura competition, used a photograph of the model, in which the negative was worked on (i.e. drawing pins turned into trees and people, boats and birds added) to give an illusion of reality to the scheme.

Reports

Reports are usually very limited (i.e. a restricted number of A4 typed sheets), but as they have to be read by several assessors it is worth presenting them in an easily handled form — for instance between two sheets of card, or, in the case of a brief report, mounted on to the boards containing the rest of the submission.

The RIBA suggests that the assessors consider asking for brochures of competition schemes consisting of the written reports and drawings reduced to A4 size so that they can study the schemes in greater depth.

One of the cheapest and easiest ways to produce a brochure for this purpose is to collect the information together, produce two cards for the covers and take it to a printer to have a spiral binding put on. There are printers who will do this on a one-off basis. The information can appear in a variety of techniques — for instance, typed or xeroxed copy, photographically reduced or xerox-reduced drawings or dyelines. If nothing is stated to the contrary, it is also possible to include folded sheets to show longer plans or sections. An acetone cover could be added to protect the brochure.

Responsibility for designs

The promoter does not undertake responsibility for the safety of competitors' drawings while they are in his care. The standard clause (taken from the RIBA Model Forms of Condition) states

"The promoter will exercise all reasonable care but will not be

31

responsible for loss or damage to drawings which may occur either in transit or during exhibition, storage or packing....."

No specific mention is made of models or any material other than in drawings but this clause could probably be held to cover all sections of a competition entry. The standard competition conditions require competitors to keep duplicates of the designs submitted. Where a model is submitted, which has some value for the competitor, it would be wise to insure it for the period it is in the hands of the promoter or in transit. Where a model is retained for exhibition, a promoter might consider arranging insurance cover, if requested to do so by a competitor.

5 Legal and professional aspects of competitions

Legal basis of the competition system in the UK
As explained in Chapter 1 the RIBA exercises control over members' competitive work through its Code of Professional Conduct. The RIBA has no legal right to stop clients inviting architects to prepare designs in competition for a particular project but does have the right, under its Charter, to require members to abide by the Code and to charge a member who contravenes the Code with "professional misconduct". As most architects are members, the RIBA does in effect have considerable control over open competition between architects. Although the Institute's *Regulations for the Promotion and Conduct of Competitions* are not enforceable by law, the conditions which the promoter will be bound to issue in accordance with these regulations, if the competition is to be given RIBA approval, become legally binding as a contract between the promoter and the competitors, taken up by a competitor registering for a competition and submitting a design.

As far as the law is concerned, it is the conditions as issued by the promoter and not the RIBA regulations on which they are based which bind the promoter. For this reason the RIBA has drawn up model forms of conditions, the wording of which must be strictly followed by promoters if the competition is to be given approval. But the general conditions in the document issued by the promoter should be very carefully read by competitors. The RIBA has been reorganising the system quite considerably in recent years, with a tendency toward giving more flexibility to the promoter, so some of the clauses which competitors take for granted — such as outright appointment of the winning architect — may not be worded in quite the way the competitor has come to expect. Even if an architect feels that the conditions for a particular competition as approved by the RIBA are not in accordance with the regulations, the conditions form the legal basis for the competition once they have been issued by the promoter and taken up by the competitor.

Eligibility

The eligibility for any particular competition will be stated in detail in the general conditions issued by the promoter, and an indication of those eligible to compete should normally be given in the press announcements. Competitions can be very varied in their entry requirements: from an ideas competition which might be open to the general public to a competition limited by invitation or locality or one in which an initial selection will be made on the basis of the experience of the intending competitors. Before embarking on the design work, it is advisable to check the invitation and the clauses on eligibility in the conditions very carefully, and if these clauses appear in any way ambiguous, to write to the promoter for guidance. This will force the promoter to take a decision in consultation with the assessors and once made it will be binding, giving a competitor a written assurance that he can enter, which cannot be set aside at a later date. Such a check should be made well before any schemes are submitted.

Acceptance of the registration fee by the promoter does not usually constitute recognition of the competitor as a bona fide entrant. Most promoters check qualifications and eligibility in detail only when the envelopes are opened after the competition has been judged or when the first-stage selection has been made. The design of a competitor who proves to have been ineligible will then be set aside. The promoter is not bound to make any formal statement about this. A number of people do submit designs for competitions for which they are not eligible and on at least one occasion a competition was "won" by an architect who had no right to compete. As well as being a waste of time for the competitor concerned, it is also bad for the competition system, as a promoter has to accept as winner a design which he knows to have been judged "second best".

As with all the clauses which make up the general conditions, the clause on eligibility for each particular competition means exactly what it says and not what people think it might have said had the promoter been more logical, broadminded, understanding or sensible. As a general rule, ideas competitions are open to architects and students of architecture, and project competitions — where there is an undertaking to appoint the winning architect as architect for the job or where such an appointment might result — are open to architects only, often, in the case of UK competitions, with a limitation that they be resident or practising in the United Kingdom.

The word "architect", in this context, means any person who at the time of his application for the competition conditions and of submission of the competition entry is registered under the Architects'

(Registration) Acts 1931 to 1969, or, being qualified for registration, has already made an application to the Architects' Registration Council (ARCUK) to be admitted to the Register. In two-stage project competitions students may be permitted to enter the first stage provided that they undertake to form an association with a registered architect if they are selected to go forward to the second stage. This is an extension to the standard eligibility for project competitions and is only included if the promoter so wishes. In ideas competitions the definition of "student" is often fairly loose and can be taken as applying to anyone following a recognised course of architecture at a university or polytechnic, including people who are working for a year halfway through their courses. For the purposes of entering the first stage of a project competition the word "student" is, in the UK, closely defined as "an RIBA student member", which means that the competitor would have to have reached intermediate level.

Eligibility is one of the aspects of competitions which varies most from one country to another. It depends on the structure of the profession within a country, the jurisdiction of the institute concerned and the traditions of the country. In Finland, for instance, competitions are open to all Finnish citizens whether they are architects or not, whereas in Switzerland, entry can be restricted by canton, parish or even religious belief. In all competition systems (including that of the RIBA) the regulations give only the limits of eligibility. For specific competitions, would-be competitors have to refer to the published conditions.

Group entries

If a team of people want to enter a competition it is usually sufficient if one member of the team fulfils the entry requirements. In Britain, any such association should, of course, not be inconsistent with the RIBA or ARCUK codes so far as members are concerned.

Multidisciplinary teams can be built up including planners, engineers, quantity surveyors, sociologists, economists or anyone who has any skills to offer, provided that the member of the team who is eligible to compete within the terms of the conditions is the registered competitor and the entry is submitted in his name. The other names may be included on the registration form and entry form and these people will be credited with the design in the eventual publicity but if, for any reason, the competitor who fulfils the entry requirements leaves the team during the progress of a competition, that team will no longer be able to compete. If a number of people in a group fulfil the eligibility requirements, registration may be transferable, although it

35

is advisable to check with the promoter if the entry is to be submitted in any name other than that of the registered competitor.

In all cases if a number of people are entering a competition as a group, they should establish, right at the outset, the basis on which the entry will be made. Small groups of people often start developing the design for a competition, consult their friends, and get some help in drawing up and generally working out the scheme in a fluid situation in which many people have participated. They are then amazed to find that these people still want to be involved when there is prize money to be shared out or the chance of a commission. In the promoter's interest, all entry forms require competitors to sign a statement which reads "It was necessary for us to form an association for the purpose of entering this competition" and "We declare that a partnership agreement is in existence for the purpose of carrying out the project in the event of the association winning the competition." (The first sentence may be deleted if an association is already established.)

Drawing up an agreement
There is no set form for the drawing up of an agreement between individuals for the purpose of entering a competition. In a small competition where there is no possibility of a commission resulting, it is probably sufficient for the basis of the association to bet set out in a document as agreed by all those concerned and to be signed and a copy given to each of the signatories. This should state whether all are equal parties in the design and should cover such things as how any prize money is to be shared, who is to be credited with the design, who owns the copyright and how the costs are to be borne. A paper such as this will be valid as a legal agreement and will fulfil the requirements of the standard entry form referred to above. In a larger competition or a project competition and certainly in the second stage of a competition, a group of individuals who have got together to submit an entry should consult a solicitor for advice on drawing up the terms of the association. These should cover not only the basis on which the entry is worked out and submitted but also the possibility of the association winning the competition and being commissioned to carry out the project, in which case a formal partnership can be established along the lines set out in the document of association for the competition. A solicitor's advice should also be sought as to the terms of this partnership agreement.

Forming an association with an established practice
One of the aspects of the competition system which worries many

promoters is the fear that the winning design will be the work of a young architect who, in spite of his talent, has had very little experience of getting the project off the drawing board and on to the ground. To guard against this eventuality, RIBA project competitions carry a clause which states:

> *"The author of the selected design may be required to satisfy the assessors that he has the resources to carry out the work efficiently. If they are not satisfied that he possesses or can develop a suitable organisation they may, at their discretion, after consultation with the author of the selected design advise the promoter that a second architect should be appointed to collaborate with the author of the selected design in carrying out the work, but without obligation on the promoters to pay any additional fees. The assessors will be prepared if necessary to assist the author of the selected design and the second architect in agreeing a suitable apportionment of the fees which could otherwise be due to the former".*

Although many competition systems have a safeguard of this sort, assessors have been very unwilling to take up this option in the past and there is no recent case of an association of this type having been formed on the insistence of the assessors. Young architects have, however, voluntarily formed associations with more experienced firms to handle large projects. After the adverse publicity given to the problems arising from some recent competitions in the UK, assessors may well feel that such an association protects the less experienced architect and gives confidence to the client. If a young team do find themselves in this situation and do not have any definite ideas as to which practice to associate with, the assessors would be able to give them advice and in Britain the RIBA Clients' Advisory Service would be able to provide a shortlist of suitable firms and would help make the necessary approaches. With regard to the legal aspects of forming an association at this stage, the services of a solicitor would be required.

There is no material published by the RIBA about forming an association either for entering a competition or setting up in practice. However, RIBA Services Ltd retains a solicitor with experience in this field and his services are available to members, through RIBA Services Ltd, on a fee-paying basis.

Architects' copyright
The regulations and standard conditions for all UK competitions state that "the ownership of copyright in the work of all competitions will

be in accordance with the Copyright Act 1956". Section 3(1) of this Act defines "artistic works" as

"a work of any of the following descriptions:
a) the following, irrespective of artistic quality, namely paintings, sculptures, drawings, engravings and photographs, and
b) works of architecture, being either buildings or models for buildings".

Copyright therefore exists both in the architect's plans and in the buildings erected from the plans. The general rule is that copyright in plans belongs to the architect unless there is an agreement to the contrary.

(A more detailed description of copyright in plans and buildings can be found in William H. Gill, *Rimmer's The Law Relating to the Architect*, Stevens, 1964, which should be read in conjunction with Keith Manson's article "Architects' Copyright" in the October 1971 issue of the *RIBA Journal*, from which the above definition is taken.)

In competitions the payment of prize money does not entitle the promoter to make any use of the winning or premiated designs other than publishing or exhibiting them for bona fide publicity purposes connected with the particular competition. The standard conditions state "The premiated designs may by agreement be retained for a further period by the promoter for the purposes of exhibition, publicity and illustrations, subject always to the provisions of Clause 10" (i.e. the clause on copyright quoted above). In ideas or planning competitions a clause is sometimes inserted to suggest that the promoter might wish to negotiate with the authors of the premiated designs for the right to implement these designs in whole or in part, but the terms are always left to the competitor to arrange to his own satisfaction. In RIBA approved competitions no competitor relinquishes any of his legal rights of copyright on the designs he submits by entering the competition. This is not always the case in international competitions where there is a system of "special purchase" of some winning designs (see Chapter 10).

Income tax on prize money
There is no accepted official ruling which states categorically that the prize money won in architectural competitions is liable to income tax in the United Kingdom, but most decisions which have been made in the past suggest that it is. In most cases the first prize in a competition carries with it an appointment which results in a professional fee being

paid to the winner. The prize money is deducted from this fee and so, in effect, becomes part of the assessable profits of the architect in question. As to the winner of the second or third prize, it could be assumed that he entered the competition to get the first prize, which looked at in this way is assessable, so that any profit he makes from this effort to secure the first prize would be equally assessable.

Some years ago, the RIBA sought a clarification of the position as regards tax liability and received a letter from HM Inspector of Taxes, Welbeck District, dated 6 April 1954, which reads as follows:

"With further reference to our recent correspondence in connection with competition awards to architects, this matter has been carefully considered by my head office and I am instructed that in the official view prizes won in an architectural competition by architects in practice are liable under Case 11 of Schedule D, being regarded as professional receipts, liable to tax."

The RIBA has more recently asked for advice on this matter from its accountants and they state that they can see no valid reason for challenging the 1954 ruling:

"I would assume that the situation covered by the above case is where a firm of architects or a practising architect has entered for a competition and used his office facilities and staff for the purpose of preparing the necessary plans. If a prize was won then it would be taxable after expenses had been charged to the business, conversely if no prize was won the expenses would still be chargeable as business expenses."

The situation of a salaried architect who enters competitions in his spare time is less clear. There is some evidence to suggest that the prize money is regarded as money which the architect receives through the practice of his profession and is therefore taxable. There are also grounds for arguing that it is not part of an architect's business to enter competitions and that the prize money is therefore "casual profit" and not "freelance earnings". In an ideas competition with no chance of a commission, there would be a much stronger case for treating the prize money in this way, particularly if the competition were open to members of the general public, but it would be up to the individual concerned to argue the particular situation on its merits. However, if a salaried architect made a habit of entering competitions, it would be open for the revenue to attack him on the basis that he was running a "professional activity", although in this case he might be able to claim expenses on all competitions he entered, whether he won a prize or not, against the Schedule D'income.

RIBA members and publicity
Competitions of all types offer architects valuable opportunities for publicity, either on their own account or for their practice. In taking advantage of these opportunities, members should be aware of the provision of the Code of Professional Conduct in this respect. Generally speaking, members are not permitted to send unsolicited material to the non-technical press or the media but are allowed to respond to invitations to write, talk or have their work featured. The *RIBA Journal* carried a useful practice note on public relations, copies of which are available from the RIBA Bookshop: "Members and Public Relations", *RIBA Journal*, May 1973.

6 Working with consultants

Consultants and the competition system

Architectural competitions involve not only architects but many other specialists and designers, either as part of a multidisciplinary team or as consultants. In recent years conditions for RIBA competitions have tended to encourage the multidisciplinary approach and entry qualifications have changed from "architects" to "teams led by an architect" and now to "teams which include an architect". There have also been in Britain competitions sponsored jointly by a number of professional institutes (such as the River Clyde Ideas and Study competition, promoted by the Corporation of Glasgow in 1973, with the cooperation of the RIBA, the RTPI and the ILA) and more broadly based competitions which have been open to the general public (for instance, the RIBA Annual Conference competitions). Even in the most specific architectural project competitions, other professions are often closely involved with the production of the entry. Nearly all the architects questioned who had had some success in competitions worked with a quantity surveyor on the competition entry and, in many cases, engineers were also brought into the team. Which consultants are used for any one competition, depends, of course, on the nature of the job but recent competition entries have involved structural, electrical and mechanical engineers, heating, lighting and ventilation consultants, civil and traffic engineers, landscape architects and engineers, economic consultants, theatre project consultants and museum experts, acoustics consultants, as well as graphic artists and modelmakers. Some of these would have been members of the design team right from the start while others would have been consulted only on specific aspects of the design. In most cases people from other professions will join with the architects in preparing a scheme on a competitive basis, although this may not always be in line with the policies of their particular professional organisations.

Quantity surveyors

About 80% of the architects questioned said they used the services of quantity surveyors on most of the competitions they entered. Without exception the quantity surveyors entered with the architects on a speculative basis though there was normally an understanding that if the architect was commissioned for the job, the QS would be appointed. The RIBA encourages promoters to leave the appointment of consultants open in the competition situation, but because some clients wish to use their own consultants or the ones with whom they normally work, it should not be taken for granted that the architect is in a position to make a recommendation.

Although young architects tend to go to their contemporaries in other professions, this is not always the wisest course. There are advantages to getting help from an established firm, which will have had considerably more experience of the problems that face an architect away from the drawing board and will probably know quite a lot more about the competition system. Established firms will take on young architects, not least because the architects who have the energy and initiative to spend time on competitions are the ones most likely to bring in commissions in the future. Some QSs are obviously more competition minded than others but it should not be difficult for a young architect to find someone who is prepared to advise on the costs aspect of his scheme.

A large firm known to be sympathetic to this sort of work may already be working on the brief with other competitors. This is not seen as a problem as it does not lead to the copying of ideas but gives the QS a chance to build up expertise from which everybody will gain. In any case a QS would always tell a client if he were already working on another scheme for the same competition. As far as an international competition is concerned an established firm of quantity surveyors will often have links with overseas countries and be able to give valuable advice on such things as building regulations (extent of services, fire and other safety requirements) and building costs, which can have a considerable effect on the design.

Quantity surveyors like to be involved at an early stage. No architect will receive a very warm welcome if he takes his entry round to get advice on how much it will cost just before the closing date. The QSs' role as they see it themselves is to guide the architect at the stage where he is considering a number of options and to steer him away from a line of development which will make the design difficult to get within the cost limits. An unadventurous QS could be a handicap and might inhibit the design; the sort of QS an intelligent architect would select would want to be part of the team and ideally should be given a chance to look at the brief and question it before the official period for questions closes. Quantity surveyors are being trained in disciplines much wider than ten years ago and the competition system gives them a welcome chance to work on situations which are free from some of the usual constraints. A large firm might well therefore give a competition to a young QS who would be backed up by a more experienced man to advise him. One of the differences in the approach to a competition project from that to a normal architect/client commission is that the architect has to take his own decisions and close his options without being able to consult the client and must do so early enough in the development of the design to be able to present a properly worked-out and viable solution. It is here that the QS sees an opportunity to make a valuable contribution.

RICS position
The regulations which govern architectural competitions in Britain are drawn up by the RIBA and are not officially accepted by any other professional institutes as far as their codes of conduct in respect of fees are concerned. However, the Royal Institute of Chartered Surveyors has always taken the view that it would be beneficial to clients and architects alike if quantity surveyors were to be involved in architectural competitions and has held discussions with the RIBA in the past on this question. The RICS feels that the RIBA has made very little effort to further these discussions, although the late Professor Bill Howell, who was a member of the Competitions Working Group at the RIBA, did set up a meeting in 1970 and organise a scheme for involving quantity surveyors in architectural competitions. This was used on an experimental basis for the Burrell competition. The RICS nominated a panel of eleven firms of chartered quantity surveyors, from which the architects invited to proceed to the second stage were requested to select one firm with which to work. The intention was that even if an inexperienced architect won the competition, the promoter could be assured that he had been given advice on the cost aspects by an established firm of quantity surveyors. It did not, however, take account of the contact many architects have with their quantity surveyors during the early stages of a competition. The Quantity Surveyors Divisional Council considered the procedure adopted in the Burrell competition but felt that in open competitions, where the number of entries was likely to be high, it would not be practical to use this procedure as it required the client to approve selected firms of quantity surveyors right from the outset. It was then suggested that the RIBA should be encouraged to include a clause in their rules on the following lines:

"The submission must be accompanied by a cost appraisal prepared by a quantity surveyor. The name of that quantity surveyor will be submitted with that of the architect."

If the RIBA were to give official recognition to quantity surveyors in this way, the RICS feels that its members would welcome the opportunity for full participation in architectural competitions and would be prepared to give urgent consideration to the question of its code of conduct in so far as fees are affected. The RIBA Competitions Working Group supports the inclusion of experienced quantity surveyors in competition teams but has not yet made any moves towards incorporating a clause along the lines suggested.

It would seem sensible from the point of view of both institutes to bring quantity surveyors officially into the competition system, as it would regulate a practice which is common in fact if not in theory and is agreed to be beneficial to competitors and promoters as well as the quantity surveyors who take part.

Engineers
There is no clear statement issued by the Association of Consulting Engineers as regards their members working with architects in UK competitions. But engineers work with architects on competition projects and are often very closely involved with the preparation of a competition scheme. The competition system gives them the opportunity to make contact with the students and young architects who will be involved in the building projects of the future and it also offers the same potential for developing ideas and exploring new techniques that attracts architects. One international engineering firm claimed that its most interesting work came from competitions. The engineers there welcomed the opportunity to work as a team and felt the "brainstorming" sessions that produced a number of different viewpoints were stimulating and constructive. They wanted to work as members of the design team and not just as specialists brought in to comment on one particular aspect and felt that they had far more to offer architect competitors who were prepared to work in this way. For this reason they preferred limited competitions, where architects were more likely to bring a multidisciplinary team together right at the outset, though as with the quantity surveyors, most competition-orientated engineering firms would be prepared to help young architects who did not have any established contacts. But engineers too object to architects who rush in at the last minute for advice when it is too late to feed anything in to the design.

Engineers are involved in fewer competitions than quantity surveyors because not all projects require their special skills; housing, for instance, makes very few demands on the engineer at the competition stage, especially since high-rise blocks have tended to be abandoned as a solution to high-density living. However, there have been many competitions in which engineering advice was required. The River Clyde Study competition, for instance, was a project which gave scope for ideas at the early stages, as a large proportion of the site was water and retaining walls, and it was necessary to establish the potential before embarking on the design. The New Parliamentary Building competition also posed structural problems on a site which was interwoven with tunnels which made the exact positioning of the load-bearing structure crucial.

One specific example of how the competition system can lead engineers into new areas of research is the requirement in two recent competition designs for inclined lifts. The design developed by Building Design Partnership for the UN City in Vienna depended on the installation of lifts at an angle, as did the prize-winning pyramid for Northampton County Council. Each competition took the engineers associated with the designs nearer to solving the problems connected with such an installation.

As far as fees are concerned, engineers, like quantity surveyors, seem to be prepared to go along with a gentleman's agreement as regards appointment if the practice wins the commission and a share on time-for-time basis of any prizes or honoraria won. With a major project (a limited competition or the second stage of an open competition) a firm may be able to allocate time within a group to work on the competition but often engineers will, like architects, work in their spare time on a competition project which interests them.

Specialist advice

For a particular building type, more specialised advice may be required, especially at the second stage. In the Burrell competition for the design of a museum to house works of art, including paintings, tapestries and old documents, both lighting and security presented problems to the competitors, and consultants were asked to advise on these aspects.

If there is an opportunity for the consultants to be appointed if the design is awarded first prize and the architect is commissioned for the job, then it is likely that they will advise competitors without requiring payment. It is difficult to give any specific information on this point as it is not strictly within the code of the institutes to which most consultants belong for members to work in this way, but no architect questioned claimed to have paid fees to any of the various consultants with whom he had worked.

Professionals involved in the presentation of the entry, such as modelmakers, artists and photographers, would expect to be paid fees for the work they do.

From the promoter's point of view, assessors may recommend that specialist advice be made available to them, depending on the nature and complexity of the particular project. This would normally be required only at the final stage of the competition and would be paid for by the promoter. (See Chapter 8, "Promoting a competition" and Chapter 9, "The work of the assessors".)

7 Winning: from the announcement of the result to setting up in practice

Once the competition entry is handed in many weeks may go by before an official envelope arrives, bearing a duplicated letter, thanking the entrants for their interest and informing them of the names of the successful competitors and the date of the exhibition. This, for 95%, is the final outcome of all the hard work that went into the competition. Why does it take so long and what happens in the case of those who actually win the competition?

From judging to announcing the result
A competition is an event which will have cost the promoter time, money and a considerable amount of effort and he will want to ensure that the result is properly presented and will get a good reception. It is unlikely therefore that he will be prepared to announce the winner without a good deal of preliminary preparation. Firstly, there are the simple mechanics to be seen to. Once the assessors have reached their final conclusion, one of them has to draft a report which has to be approved by the other members and the details of the award have to be set out and signed. The eligibility and qualifications of those submitting the winning and commended schemes have to be checked with the architectural institute or registering body to see that they fulfil the entry requirements. At this stage the promoter may well contact the winning architect but will ask him to treat the information as confidential until the formal announcement is made.

As the material submitted for a competition is so limited in scope, the winning architect will often be asked to prepare one or two perspective drawings to illustrate his scheme to the promoter's committees or associates and to the general public. Where a project is likely to attract a lot of public interest he may also be asked to prepare a model. At this stage, the restrictions on presentation are no longer valid and the competitor can produce any material he wishes to explain and present his scheme. The costs of material specifically requested by the promoter will be paid but any additional material the competitor himself wishes to produce must be financed out of the prize money.

47

During the period between the assessment and the announcement of the results the promoter, with the advice of the assessors and often the professional institute concerned, will be preparing a press release and planning the presentation ceremony. There are two main ways of handling the press release: the promoter may decide to release the results to the press well before the official announcement with an embargo on publication before a given date, or he may decide to send an invitation to a presentation ceremony when the results are announced and material handed out to the press. The former course has the advantage that the press are able to cover the results while the exhibition is still on (the presentation ceremony and announcement of the results usually takes place at the opening of the exhibition), and are given time to collect material and search out additional information before publication which gives a better coverage to the competition. If the promoter decides to handle the announcement in this way, it is likely that members of the press will contact the winner and runners-up to ask for copies of their drawings and reports. It is quite in order to supply these, provided that the press are made aware of any embargo which might exist.

The presentation ceremony
Promoters will usually organise some sort of function at which the prize money is presented, often planned to coincide with the opening of the exhibition and a press conference. Where the results have already been given to the press, it will be very much a social affair but if the information has been held back, the winning competitors can expect a lot of press interest. Publicity-minded architects may want to distribute their own press handouts, in addition to those prepared by the promoter, giving more information about the scheme and about the members of their team. Provided certain guidelines are followed, there is nothing unethical about this and it can help to increase the coverage of the competition by supplying the press with more varied information. Pictures are also welcome, but reduced copies of the competition entries are rarely much use (except to the technical press), as grey and white plans have little public appeal and any explanatory text becomes too small to read. A simple perspective view, strong enough to have some impact when reduced to one newspaper column width, is more acceptable. Local radio stations also take an interest in competition results and will often send a reporter to the presentation ceremony. It is therefore advisable to brief one member of the group who enjoys being interviewed. The publicity need not necessarily all go to the winner on this occasion; in fact there are several cases where

the winner has got the job but the runner-up has taken most of the glory. Local press and radio will often follow up a local competitor, even if he is not among the main prize winners.

When the presentation ceremony is held after the results have been made public, it becomes more of a social event and gives the winning competitor a chance to explain his scheme to those who will decide whether or not it goes ahead.

The exhibition
Once the results are made public, the promoter is committed to arranging an exhibition of entries both to give competitors the opportunity of seeing the winning designs and to publicise the results. This is a valuable part of the competition system as it allows people to study the alternative solutions, to assess the jury's work and to see how the architectural profession has responded to the demands of the particular brief. However, where the competition attracts a large response, the exhibition causes problems. For instance, a slow walk round the exhibition of entries for the Amsterdam City Hall international competition took over four hours, without stopping to study any of the designs in detail. The RIBA has, to a certain extent, opted out of the problem by requiring only the second-stage designs to be shown in a two-stage competition but this is not a very satisfactory solution. It causes bitterness amongst other competitors who, quite justifiably, resent the fact that after all their effort, nobody has the chance to see their work. It also goes against the spirit of competitions in that the fairness of the decision is not made fully apparent when so many schemes are not shown to the public and the opportunity which should be offered for research into the alternative solutions is lost. The RIBA Competitions Group hopes to persuade assessors to make a long shortlist of twenty or thirty schemes which can be "commended for exhibition" so that a wider range of entries can be shown than the six or seven second-stage designs promoters are asked to exhibit at present.

Where a number of competitions are regularly in progress, the entries are dispersed and the problem of exhibiting them is thus made easier. In the meantime, competitors in countries where there are few competitions may have to accept that their designs will not get the publicity they should receive.

At international exhibitions there is usually an attempt to show all the entries. However, some promoters add to competitors' difficulties by opening the exhibition at the same time as they announce the results without giving prior warning to competitors, the national sections of the International Union of Architects, or the press, with the obvious result that very few competitors outside the immediate area ever get the chance to see the entries. Competition exhibitions very rarely tour, so competitors who are unable to attend the first showing will probably not be given another opportunity (though in the UK the RIBA does try to make sure that if an exhibition takes place outside London, the winning designs at least are shown at its headquarters in Portland Place). This is partly because of the expense of setting up the exhibition but also because of the obligation to return all entries to competitors within a set period after the results have been announced.

Appointment of the winning architect
All RIBA project competitions carry with them, in some form or other, a commitment on the part of the promoter to appoint the winning architect. In the standard single-stage or two-stage competition, this is a straightforward commitment to appoint the architect of the design placed first by the assessors as architect for the work, but it may be a commitment to appoint the winning architect (possibly alongside one or two other second-stage or selected competitors) to carry out further studies, as in the Preliminary Project competitions, or it could be only a commitment to appoint the architect of one of several designs selected by the assessors, as in the Promoter Choice competition. This is as far as the competition regulations take the promoter and the architect in the UK. Once the architect is formally appointed, in accordance with the standard form of contract published by the RIBA, the normal client/architect relationship is established and the assessors have no further jurisdiction. Normal scale fees are paid and the prize money the architect received is merged with these fees.

Proof of ability to carry out the work
The RIBA system, in line with those of several other organisations, requires the assessors to satisfy themselves that the winning architect has the resources to carry out the work efficiently. They are obliged to interview the winning architect and to find out what work he has done either in his own capacity or as an employee, and what level of experience he has gained in supervising a job and in taking a client's instructions. If the winning architect is employed by an existing practice or a public authority, the assessors may well contact the partners or principal, to find out what level of responsibility he has undertaken and what their opinion was of his ability to carry out the

job on his own. If he is recommended to form an association, the choice of collaborator would be left to him, although suggestions might be made by the assessors. (See Chapter 5, "Legal and professional aspects of competitions".)

Non-appointment of the architect or abandonment of the project
Although the RIBA regulations "require" the promoter to state that it is his intention to build and appoint the winning architect to do the work, in some cases the promoter is either unwilling or unable to do so. RIBA regulations 34 to 41 cover this contingency. They state that, if a promoter fails to appoint the winning architect or gives him no instructions to proceed with the work within a period of two years from the announcement of the award, the architect will be paid an additional fee of the same amount as the premium originally paid to him as author of the design placed first (i.e. his prize money will be doubled). If the architect is appointed and given instructions but the job, for some reason, does not proceed, the architect is then paid normal scale fees for the amount of work he has done. If these fees amount to less than double the first premium, he still has the right to claim this amount.

Once the promoter has compensated the winning architect in the prescribed way, he has no further commitment to him or to any other competitor.

(The promoter's commitment to the winning architect is one of the factors which varies most in the different systems. The RIBA system tends to be one which encourages the promoter to commit himself to building the winning scheme.)

Setting up in practice as the result of a competition
One of the main attractions of competitions to young architects is the opportunity to set up in practice long before they could hope to achieve this in any other way.

Considering the number of competitions there have been over the years in the UK, the list of practices which owe their inception or growth to the competition system is quite impressive. Powell and Moya were still in their middle twenties when they won the Pimlico Housing competition directly after the war. Philip Powell (now Sir Philip Powell) in turn helped the practice of Darbourne and Darke to get started when, as an assessor for the Lillington Street Housing Scheme competition, he selected John Darbourne's entry as the winner. Now, nearly fifteen years later, this practice is regarded both in the UK and abroad as one of the leading teams of housing architects.

John Darbourne is still only at an age when many architects, without a competition win, would be just starting in practice. In the forties and fifties names such as Eric Lyons; the Grenfell Baines Group of Architects; Alison and Peter Smithson; Leonard Manasseh; Gollins, Melvin and Ward; Chamberlin, Powell and Bon and, of course, Basil Spence (now Sir Basil Spence) appeared amongst the lists of competition winners. Casson and Conder were also brought together through the competition system, and, in the sixties, practices such as Hutchinson, Locke and Monk; Evans and Shalev; Neylan and Ungless; Theakstone and Duell; Boissevain and Osmond; Ahrends, Burton and Koralek and the Goad Burton Partnership were all started, to some extent, through winning a competition.

A study of UK competition prizewinners over the last two or three decades shows that a single competition win does not necessarily guarantee a successful future, and many of the architects listed above worked on several competitions, sometimes picking up a second or third prize, before they eventually came out top. In fact, as many practices have probably been set up through the partners finding they could work together in preparation for a competition as have been established through an actual win.

A large competition win may seem a very attractive way of setting up in practice but most architects who started in this way, though appreciating the opportunities it gave them, will confirm that it can bring problems. Not the least of these is getting jobs other than the one competition scheme. There is a tendency among clients to think that any architect who has got a prestige job will not be interested in small day-to-day buildings. On the other hand, the clients with larger commissions are going to wait to see the end result before placing work in the hands of a newly established team. One practice which was set up after winning a very large civic complex competition had to wait seven years before another client came through its doors, and, at one point, the partners went back to teaching to finance the office so that the competition project could be completed. Another group of young architects spent ten years on the single large housing project which they won as the result of an open competition, occasionally taking part in other competitions to give a little relief when the project was at its most routine stages.

Once the job is complete, it seems that clients are impressed by a competition-winning building and are keen to give it publicity and show other people around. If a young practice survives these early stages, then there are good opportunities to expand and progress. But the years in between, though rewarding, can be tough, with all the partners' time and effort going into one big job when other young architects are gaining more varied experience. The architect who sets up in practice in his twenties is also at a disadvantage because his contemporaries have not yet reached positions of authority in the organisations which are commissioning architects and so the useful "students together" link does not exist.

The best sort of competition win for a young architect who wants to start his own practice is probably a medium-sized project, without too much political significance, which he can get on with and build within a few years — although it is fair to say that of the teams which went through the difficult process of building a multimillion pound scheme as their first job, none questioned would have missed the experience. As far as the promoters were concerned, the architects felt they had been well served because of the absolute commitment they had been given with this first important commission.

Help and advice
On the whole, people who take part in competitions — from the promoter and the assessors to the other competitors — are keen to see the winning design successfully carried out. Young groups can take advantage of this interest and willingness to help and ease the process of getting the project through to completion. For instance, with the Plateau Beaubourg Arts Centre project in Paris, which Piano and Rogers won as the result of an open international competition, the architects kept in touch with the assessors, who gave them a lot of help in carrying out the scheme as originally conceived. About eighteen months after the architects were appointed and work had started on site, the jury — which included Philip Johnson, Oscar Niemeyer and Jean Prouvé — was formally invited by the client to return to discuss the scheme with the architects and the client's representatives, and this meeting helped to smooth out any difficulties which had arisen and to maintain the integrity of the competition-winning design. The architects feel that "it would be most valuable if this were established as a principle in all competitions". Although this does not appear to be standard procedure in RIBA or other competitions, there is no reason why such meetings should not take place and most assessors would be happy to act in this way.

The RIBA is also aware of the difficulties competition winners have in attracting other commissions in the early stages and the Clients' Advisory Service will nominate them for jobs where appropriate. The service cannot, of course, guarantee jobs and it always gives clients a list of four or five suitable practices which they can talk to before making their choice. But it is also the policy of the RIBA to encourage newly formed competition-winning practices both through the CAS and by including them in limited and Regional Special Category competitions.

One thing which is assured through winning a competition is publicity, though architects are divided about the value of this in terms of future commissions. However, it is worth taking advantage of what opportunities there are and keeping local societies and the professional institute informed of the progress of the project.

The building record of competition winners

Having got to the position of winning a competition what are the chances of seeing the project built? Provided it is not a "prestige project", the probability of a scheme going ahead is still high.

An analysis of RIBA-approved competitions promoted in the UK between 1960 and 1970 shows that 80% of all project competitions resulted in the winning architect being appointed and the design being built, figures which are in line with experience in Germany and in Scandinavia. Since 1970, the UK record has been much worse but still not as bad as has been claimed.

Between 1970 and 1974 there were nineteen project competitions, one of which was abandoned at the end of the first stage because of difficulties in acquiring the site. Of the remaining eighteen, the winning design was accepted by the promoting body in fifteen cases and the architect appointed in fourteen. By the middle of 1975, a building had been completed or had started on site in ten cases. (These figures exclude the two successful Regional Special Category competitions.) This means that only three competitions were rejected out of hand by the promoters.

The four schemes which were accepted but have not yet started to be built are well known: The New Parliamentary Building, The Burrell Museum, The Northampton County Hall and the Architects' Benevolent Society Homes. What is less well known is that even in the present difficult economic times, the chances of a winning scheme actually being built remain at about 60%, with those requiring special finance outside the normal budget of the promoters, being the most vulnerable.

8 Promoting a competition

A thriving competition system.needs promoters who have confidence in the results it produces and are prepared to use it. Whatever the enthusiasm of architects and their professional institutes, if promoters are not attracted to the system there will be no competitions.

The role of the competition
But what is the role of the competition system as far as the promoter is concerned? On one side there are architects, with experience and ideas as to how the built environment should be designed, but dependent on getting a client who wants a particular type of building before they can give form to their ideas. On the other hand is the client, with a brief for a project and looking for an architect to interpret and shape his requirements into built form. The client can, of course, go direct to an architect whose work he knows and respects, and place the commission in his hands. They will then work together, developing a design in accordance with the client's instructions, until the project is complete. This is the normal procedure and the one which produces most of the privately financed and many of the publicly financed buildings we see around us. Alternatively the client could decide to promote a competition.

What a competition offers a promoter is the opportunity to research a building project, discovering skills and approaches which might not normally come to his attention. This research is undertaken by a wide cross-section of the architectural profession in accordance with stated requirements set out in the promoter's brief, which forms part of the conditions issued to all competitors. The competition system is a way of regulating and ordering this work so that all parties are given both incentives and safeguards and are guided in a method which long experience has shown to produce the best results. A competition may produce general ideas on a topic of interest, approaches to a particular problem or a worked-out design for a specific building, depending on the needs and wishes of the promoter.

Whenever building work is being undertaken, a competition, in one form or another, can be considered as one of the ways of getting a design and an architect to carry it out. In short, provided a promoter is prepared to accept the basic principles of the competition system, there is no type of building which is inherently unsuitable for a competition.

For very small projects, such as a one-off family house, going out to competition would be regarded as rather overambitious but with small groups of housing, particularly in difficult or sensitive areas, competitions have been successfully promoted and have attracted a good entry. (For example, a single-stage competition was held in the southern region of the RIBA for the design of five family houses which fitted in scale and character into the surrounding village. Sixty-five schemes were submitted, giving a wide choice of solution to a tricky infill problem.) At the other end of the scale, you will hear it said that large, specialised buildings are not suitable for competitions, but this is not necessarily so. (One of the largest competitions for a single building to be held in the UK in recent years was for a Medical Teaching Centre for Wales — an £8m job even at 1960 prices — and this was given a special commendation in the 1974 RIBA Architecture Awards.) It is also said that competitions cause problems in the case of buildings where the plans of some areas cannot be made public, but the new Manchester District Bank headquarters and the Czechoslovakian Embassy in London were award-winning competition schemes.

That architects are willing to enter competitions is not in question; no country has reached a saturation point where the profession ceases to respond, even with 300 or 400 competitions a year. Nor can it be argued that the best architects do not bother with competitions or use them only to become established. Where opportunities exist architects will take them up: Arne Jacobsen, for instance, went in for competitions for as long as he practised, setting high standards of design for public architecture in Denmark, and Alvar Aalto entered at least sixty competitions during his career.

The response of architects to recent competitions shows that ideas, skill and enthusiasm are not in short supply. The competition system provides a promoter with a method of drawing on these assets within the profession if he chooses to do so. Promoting a competition is not the easiest way of getting a design for a building (the easiest way is to copy something which has been done reasonably successfully elsewhere, but in times of rapid economic and social change even this method cannot be guaranteed), but for a promoter who wants his design problem thought out fully and is prepared to accept new ideas if they are shown to be practical, a competition can provide a good, economic solution. It may even produce one of those milestones in

56

design which will ensure architect and owner a place in history, but this is an added bonus. A design which answers the promoter's requirements with competence and imagination will satisfy most promoters and this is what a competition sets out to achieve. Properly conducted, it should do so.

Information on the competition system

To get information on organising competitions in any country, an intending promoter should go to the appropriate institute or architectural organisation. There is now such a range of options that few architects will really be in a position to advise clients adequately. Thus, in the UK a client should first read the RIBA *Regulations for the Promotion and Conduct of Competitions* (included in the appendices to this book; also available free from the RIBA) and make sure he understands the basic principles of competitions and is prepared to accept the underlying requirements of the system.

Once the basic system is understood the best place to go for guidance is the RIBA. The Competitions Office will supply information on how different competitions are organised (the summary of how the system works in Chapter 2 of this book will give an indication of the number of alternatives, but it should not be taken as an exhaustive list of the options open to a particular promoter) and the Clients' Advisory Service will give advice on various ways of selecting an architect and on whether a competition is likely to be the best way of approaching the problem.

But if it is established RIBA policy to expand and support competitions, is the advice given not likely to be biased? The promoter will be told of the advantages but he will also be given information on what his commitments will be and a fair indication of the amount of time, money and effort involved. The RIBA does not appreciate unsuccessful competitions any more than the promoters concerned, so there is no reason why it should persuade someone to go out to competition if it is not thought likely to produce a good result. There are also lists of past competitions available from the RIBA, so a would-be promoter could, if he wished, contact someone in a similar position who had been responsible for organising a competition, and find out the pros and cons on the basis of his experience.

What is a promoter committed to when he organises a competition?

The basic commitment on the part of the promoter in the UK is to the *Regulations for the Promotion and Conduct of Competitions*, which have to be accepted if a competition is organised involving members of the RIBA. (See Chapter 1 for exceptions and for competitions under the jurisdiction of UIA.) What this actually means depends on the type of competition a promoter decides to hold. Where there is no intention to build, the promoter's only commitment is to accept the award of the assessors and to pay the prizes offered. (This does not, however, entitle him to use any of the schemes which are still protected by the provisions of the copyright acts.) If he does intend to build, then he has some sort of commitment to the winning architect which varies from appointing him to carry out further studies to commissioning him for work; and if, for any reason, the job does not go ahead or the promoter is not willing to appoint the winning architect, then compensation must be paid. The compensation is usually an amount equivalent to the first prize money to be paid in addition to the prize. This is now valid for all types of competition since the compensation payable in limited competitions was reduced by the RIBA Council in February 1976. The promoter is also required to accept a jury of assessors to whom he delegates the judging of the entries. Although the promoter is encouraged to be represented on the jury, the majority of its members have to be independent architects, nominated by the President of the RIBA (see Chapter 9, "The work of the assessors").

In addition to these main points, the regulations set out what should be paid in prize money to the competitors and in fees to the assessors and how the competition is to be conducted.

What costs are involved for the promoter?
The costs of promoting a competition in Britain can be divided into three parts: there are the statutory costs laid down in the regulations to cover prizes and fees payable; then there are the expenses involved in printing the conditions, publishing the result and exhibiting the entries; and lastly, there are the day-to-day running expenses. In principle, similar costs occur in other countries.

Prizes and honoraria, assessors' fees and RIBA charge
As a very rough guide, the statutory fees and charges in a competition amount to about .5% of the project value (assuming that the winning architect is appointed and his prize money merged with his fees), but the actual amount varies with the type and size of the competition.

The prize money which has to be awarded is proportionate to the value of the project (in all except ideas competitions) and is calculated in accordance with a scale published by the RIBA. This scale is worked out so that proportionally the prize money is less for a project costing several million pounds than for a small competition. For instance, on a project of an estimated value of £5m the first prize would be £7,000 whereas on a project of an estimated value of £500,000 the first prize would be £1,500. Second and third prizes also have to be awarded and these are calculated as a proportion of the first prize (one half and one third respectively). In a two-stage competition all the second-stage competitors have to be given a certain amount of prize money to help towards the cost of preparing the entry. This money is called an honorarium and amounts to something less than the third prize and is paid to each second-stage competitor who does not receive a major prize. Similarly, in a competition where named architects are specifically invited to submit designs (a limited competition), each competitor submitting a bona fide design receives either a prize or an honorarium, in accordance with the set scale.

Where a competition offers a first prize and carries a commitment to appoint the winning architect as architect for the job, once the architect is appointed, the prize he receives is regarded as an advance of fees and merged with the total fees due.

In the recently introduced types of competitions, the prize money may be divided up differently, but it amounts in total to much the same for the same stage of design work. For instance, in a Promoter Choice competition the amount of prize money would be the same as that given for a project competition of the same value but would be divided equally among the shortlisted competitors, whereas in a Preliminary Project competition the total prize money would be less as the result would not be such a fully worked-out design.

In ideas competitions, the prize money to be paid has to be negotiated with the RIBA on the advice of the assessors. It has to be sufficient to attract a good entry and recompense the winner for the amount of work involved. A commercial organisation would be expected to offer higher prizes than a small charitable organisation, and, obviously, in a fully open competition the prizes would need to be more attractive than in a small competition, run to draw attention to a local problem or to coincide with a particular event. First prizes in ideas competitions in recent years have varied from a share out of the entry fees to £2,500.

The independent architect assessors are paid in accordance with the RIBA scale of competition costs, each one receiving an amount equal to 20% of the value of the first prize. (The RIBA recommends that two architects be appointed to judge a medium-sized competition and that architects must be in the majority. Thus, if a promoter wants to appoint two of his own representatives, there need to be three architect assessors. There are rarely more than this.) The fees for the lay assessors are a matter of negotiation between the promoter and the individual concerned. These fees are exclusive of out-of-pocket expenses (i.e. costs of travelling to meetings, overnight accommodation during the judging periods, any use made of the assessors' staff or office facilities, etc.).

None of the above costs applies to the Regional Special Category competitions, in which the only prize is the appointment of the winning architect as architect for the job, and assessors offer their services free. As the name suggests this is a special type of competition and, at the time of writing, can be used only by local authorities or other public or charitable bodies with the express approval of the President of the RIBA.

In addition to the prize money and assessors' fees, the RIBA charges a fee to cover its advisory and supervisory services. This amounts to a sum equal to 20% of the first premium. In Regional Special Category competitions it is left to the discretion of the branch or region responsible for organising the competition as to whether they make this charge. If they do it is based on a hypothetical first prize, calculated in the normal way.

Presentation costs: printing, publicity and mounting the exhibition
The costs given above are the set costs in a competition and are the only ones which can be calculated with any degree of accuracy. The other costs depend very much on the type of competition, the way the promoter wishes to present the documents, the facilities he has within his organisation and the amount of publicity he wants to give the result.

The first thing to be costed in a competition is the printing of the conditions. This is the document which sets out how the competition is organised and what the promoter's requirements are. It is sent to anyone eligible to compete who writes in response to the published invitation. The only requirements made in the regulations regarding this document are that it should be clearly presented and set out all the information the competitors need in order to submit a design. The cost of printing depends very much on the style and quality of the presentation. It does not need to be expensively produced but should be well designed and clearly set out as competitors will be influenced by the care the promoter has taken with this document. Assessors are usually prepared to advise on the presentation, and the RIBA Library has sets of conditions produced for previous competitions, available for reference.

In a limited competition the conditions can be reproduced quite cheaply, as only about a dozen copies are needed. Because the promoter can assume that the competitors will visit the site, there is no need to supply a great deal of background information. In an open competition, however, it is not unusual to get more than a thousand requests for sets of conditions, so, with this number, a special design and printing job is justified. In an open competition, the competitors will also require maps, site plans and photographs of the surrounding area. (Where ordnance survey maps are reproduced a small licence fee is payable.)

It is normal to ask competitors to pay a deposit for the conditions to help towards the cost of production and to discourage people from writing for documents when they have no real intention of entering the competition. The size of the deposit depends on the amount of material which has to be provided: in recent UK competitions it has ranged from £2 to £20. In accordance with the RIBA regulations, the deposit has to be returnable to those who decline to compete and send back the conditions by a given date, as well as to those who submit a bona fide entry. Surprisingly few people, in fact, bother to reclaim their deposit by sending back the conditions, so with an average entry of 40%, the promoter can expect to retain about half the money deposited with him (or even more in an ideas competition).

It is not necessary to spend a great deal of money informing architects that a competition is taking place. By sending out a press release to the technical press, the competition will normally be covered in the editorial pages of the main architectural magazines (a more effective method, in any case, than buying advertising space). This press release would be sent out by the RIBA, unless the promoter specifically wished to do it himself, and would be regarded as part of the supervisory service, covered by the standard fee. The main publicity costs come when the result is announced, though again it depends on the promoter as to how much of an event he wants to make of it. At the minimum, he should budget for some sort of press handout, even if it is only a series of multilithed sheets. But having gone to the trouble of promoting a competition, most people would want to make an event of the announcement of the results. In this case, promoters should budget for paying for perspective drawings, possibly a model, press photographs and the cost of some sort of presentation.

The regulations require a promoter to arrange an exhibition for a period of not less than six days. In a two-stage competition only the second stage entries must be shown (although if it is possible to show a wider range it is appreciated by competitors).

In all other types of competition the promoter is required to put all the entries on display. Exhibitions can take up a large amount of space, especially where there has been a high entry. The RIBA has large rooms and exhibition screens available for hire on a commercial basis but these need to be booked well in advance. Similarly, Building Centres throughout the UK may have space and are worth approaching as they are often interested in showing competition results, but again they need to be booked. During the school holidays, most education authorities would be prepared to make a school hall available and the fees for this are generally less than for a commercial property.

Specialist advice
Although it is the responsibility of the assessors to organise the competition, draw up the conditions and make the award, in a large or complex competition they may need further help and advice and, in accordance with the regulations, have a right to ask the promoter to make this help available. The specialist advice most frequently required is on cost and in most project competitions the promoter would be expected to appoint a quantity surveyor to advise the assessors in the final stage. Assessors may also require help with the technical aspects of judging. This could be made available either by the promoter from within his own organisation or by the assessors bringing in their own staff, in which case the promoter would be required to pay the assessors for their services on a time basis. (See Chapter 9, "The work of the assessors".)

Administration
The day-to-day organisation of a competition has to be undertaken by the promoter, although he has the assessors and the RIBA to refer to for help and advice. This day-to-day organisation includes servicing the assessors' meetings, arranging for the printing of the conditions, sending out information to competitors, collecting and processing the questions, circulating the explanatory memorandum, accepting the entries, making arrangements for the judging, and organising the presentation and the announcement of the result. In large competitions some promoters appoint a competition organiser or allocate one member of their staff to this work. A large competition could take almost two years from the first decision to contact the RIBA until the winning architect is announced and the appointment finalised, and for the whole of this period someone within the promoter's organisation should be responsible for the administration. It is not, however,

anything like a full-time job and could be carried by somebody who had a regular job to do in addition to the competition work, provided that he had adequate help at peak times and sufficient support staff to call upon for such things as sending out the conditions, collecting in the entries (this covers only one or two days as everybody leaves it to the last minute) and displaying them for the assessors. Where a promoter is an individual or charitable organisation with no back-up resources, the RIBA Competitions Office might take over some of the administrative work, though this would not be covered by the normal service charge. Running a major competition is a big job but with good assessors and RIBA help it should not be an arduous one (and certainly not boring for the individuals involved).

How long does a competition take?
Again this depends on the type of competition, the speed with which the promoter is prepared to take decisions and answer correspondence and the amount of detailed information on the brief, etc., he has available when he first approaches the RIBA or equivalent body in other countries. In short, a competition can take anything from six weeks to two years (or considerably more as in the New Parliamentary Building competition, which was first discussed in 1964 and abandoned in 1975 because of the economic situation; this, however, is an exception).

The quickest type of competition to run is the Regional Special Category competition. Provided a brief has already been drawn up, it can be organised in well under three months. However, this type of competition is a package deal designed to give a quick result in a specific situation and it should not be assumed that other types of competition can be pared down to such a time scale. Where architects are invited to take part in a competition (i.e. named architects in a limited competition) the promoter can expect them to work to a tight schedule, to visit the site and to attend a discussion meeting rather than submit written questions, all of which considerably reduce the time required for a competition. Any form of limited competition can be run in three to six months.

In an open competition the competitors have to be given time to send in for conditions after the announcement has been made. They are then given a period to study the conditions and submit questions. These have to be considered by the assessors, who prepare an explanatory memorandum which is circulated to competitors. A design period of about three full months is allowed (bearing in mind that in an open competition competitors cannot be expected to allocate a set period to working on the design and have to fit it in with their normal work). The entries are collected in and judged, checks have to be made and then the results can be announced and the winning architect appointed. In a two-stage competition, the process described above brings you only to the beginning of the second stage. A further briefing document has to be prepared and circulated to the shortlisted competitors, who are given a further three months in which to develop their designs. All this means that a single-stage competition takes about ten months and a two-stage competition about fifteen months, though some time could be cut off these estimates if a promoter were really prepared to push everything through quickly.

By making over-optimistic comparisons with the normal commissioning process, promoters should not underestimate the time that is needed. It is worth remembering that with a competition, on the given date the promoter will be able to appoint an architect on the basis of a fully worked-out and costed design. (A competition does not, however, produce working drawings, so an additional period must be added to the times given to reach tender stage.)

When should a competition be considered?
A competition is regarded in some countries as a standard method of finding an architect, particularly when the spending of public money is involved. Just as organisations in the UK will ask a number of firms to tender for the construction of a building or the provision of equipment, so many authorities in Germany and Switzerland will automatically require a number of designs to be submitted before an architect is appointed. There is no reason why this should not be the case elsewhere. Competition is as relevant in architectural design as it is in those areas of commerce and other daily activity where it is taken for granted. Putting a project out to competition will focus attention on the special needs of the particular client, while stimulating original thinking and pushing forward the boundaries of research. A competition can be used to find more economic or satisfying solutions to standard briefs or to look into new methods of design and construction.

For a public body or commercial organisation with a series of projects, competitions can be used to distribute the work on the basis of merit and to bring able new architects onto the shortlist for direct commissions. Many local authorities that have their own design departments still give some work out to private practices. For small- and medium-sized projects the Regional Special Category competition gives the opportunity to fit a competition into the normal programme of work, enabling the choice to be made from a number of local practices on the basis of a preliminary design. For larger projects, the open competition system offers the same opportunity for selection but extends the choice to the whole of the United Kingdom. Though requiring more planning, it should still be possible to fit the timetable into the rolling programme.

From the point of view of the private promoter, the competition system gives him the chance to see what the plan and architectural treatment of a particular solution will be before making a decision to appoint the architect. (Most competition designs show plans, elevations and sections, with perspective drawings of the completed scheme where this is appropriate.) In drawing up the brief and making the selection the promoter will have the guidance of the assessors. For a client with little experience of working with an architect, this assistance can be very valuable.

Competitions can also have a good public relations value. Although the political 'hot potato' project does not always work to the advantage of the competition system itself, for a promoter with a difficult project a competition can be the most open way of dealing with a problem and it will be seen that every attempt is being made to get the best solution. Where a number of different interests are involved, the difficult process of selecting one architect can be eased by placing this decision in the hands of a jury of independent assessors.

Going out to competition is also a good way of stimulating public interest in the built environment. Competitions always attract publicity and are well covered by the local press and radio from the launching to the announcement of the result. Where the winning architects have been asked to present their schemes to local people, the meetings have been well attended and the initiative welcomed.

The ideas competition can also be used to play a more important role than simply an exercise in design. Such competitions can draw attention to the potential of a site or area and can explore the possible development of a building type or construction material. (Competitions of this type can provide very inexpensive publicity. So to ensure that the system is not abused the RIBA does not give approval to competitions which are purely for advertising purposes or restricted to the use of a proprietary product.) They can also be used to study a problem which, while having extensive implications, is concerned with small individual buildings, none of which in themselves would justify a project competition or even, in some cases, the services of an architect. For instance, the problems of infill and conservation, of providing modern amenities in old buildings, of building in the countryside or in areas with a strong vernacular tradition, of what to do with land awaiting development or how to improve the design of self-help buildings, could all be the subject of ideas competitions.

Documentation
The following documents are available free from the RIBA: RIBA *Regulations for the Promotion and Conduct of Competitions*; RIBA outline timetables for the standard types of competitions; and the official chart of costs
Papers on:
Developer/Architect competitions
Preliminary Project competitions
Promoter Choice competitions
Regional Special Category competitions

9 The work of the assessors

The assessors are the key factor in the successful promotion of a competition. In Britain the RIBA sets out their duties in *Organising a Competition* as follows:

> *"Assessors are nominated by the President in consultation with the Promoter in accordance with the Regulations (see regulations 4-10). Once assessors have been appointed they are responsible for the conduct of the competition. They are required not only to judge the schemes submitted but to act as professional advisers to the Promoter in all matters relating to the competition. They may seek the advice of the RIBA Competitions Committee and call upon the services of any specialist or professional help they require but the ultimate responsibility for all decisions taken during the course of a competition rests with the assessors".*

The "conduct of the competition" extends, in effect, from confirming that the project is suitable for a competition and advising on the best way of organising it, to the assessors satisfying themselves that the winning architect is able to undertake the project and advising the promoter on the presentation of the results. It is a major commitment and can last several years.

There are basically two ways of organising the conduct of a competition: one (that recommended by the RIBA) is to make the assessors responsible right from the outset; the other (used in Switzerland, Canada and the USA, as described in Chapter 12) is to appoint a professional adviser (an architect with experience of the competition system) to draw up the conditions and organise the competition, bringing in assessors only to judge the entries and select the winning designs. The process described in this chapter is similar whichever system is used, but where a professional adviser is appointed, many of the duties described as those of the assessors will be undertaken by him.

Who chooses the assessors?

According to the RIBA regulations, assessors are nominated by the President and appointed by the promoter. What does this statement mean in practice? This depends very much on the type of competition and the promoter, but normally, once the promoter has decided to pursue the idea of a competition, he will discuss the project with representatives of the Competitions Committee at the RIBA, who will try to establish his aims and requirements. A shortlist of names of possible assessors will then be drawn up, which may well include suggestions put forward by the promoter himself. There are no established architect assessors nor even a set list from which names are selected. In fact, very few architects have been involved in assessing more than one competition and anyone who has been on a competition jury as many as three times in the last twenty years is very much an exception.

A jury is usually made up of between two and four independent architects and one or two lay assessors, representing the promoter. Assessors are selected very much as a jury, rather than as a collection of eminent individuals. The sort of factors taken into consideration are their experience in the particular field of the competition, the respect they have in the profession, their appeal to a wide range of architects including younger members, compatibility with the promoting body and the confidence that body will have in their judgement and the experience they have of the competition system. Wherever possible, a balanced jury will be created with no definite "style" indicated by the names chosen, unless the promoter has given a definite preference for a particular approach. The final selection will be made by the RIBA President, on the advice of the Competitions Committee. Assessors are bound to be establishment figures to the extent that their names and work must be known to a fair cross-section of the profession, but a look at the people who have assessed competitions over the past fifteen or so years will show quite a wide range of architectural approach, background (public authority, private practice and academic), age and "eminence". The one discernible bias is that in favour of architects who have themselves had success in the competition system.

Lay assessors

One of the changes made by the RIBA in its last major revision of the competition system in 1968 was the introduction of lay assessors on to the judging panel. The term "lay" is rather a misnomer as, in the context of the competition regulations, it means that the assessor is selected by the promoter to represent his interests. In fact, the chief architect to a government department, New Town architects and county architects have all acted as lay assessors in recent competitions, as have a director of housing and a chairman of a planning committee. Most architect assessors welcome the inclusion on the juries of people who are specifically chosen to represent the promoter's point of view, whether they are other architects or interested laymen. They find the lay assessors make a particularly valuable contribution to the preparation of the conditions, as they have local knowledge and are aware of the individual requirements, or even prejudices, of the promoter, and provide invaluable help in explaining the winning scheme to the promoting body. In spite of one well-publicised case of an architect/layman split, most joint juries reach a unanimous verdict, and in such cases there is a very good chance that the project will be well received and that the winning architect will get a chance to proceed with the job (economic situation permitting).

The first duties of the assessors
Although a promoter will have discussed his project with the RIBA in some detail before assessors are appointed, it is the responsibility of the assessors to determine whether the project is suitable for a competition and, if so, how it should be organised. Assessors very rarely fail to recommend holding a competition, because the system is sufficiently flexible to cover most situations where the promoter is willing to accept the basic principles. However, assessors, once they have visited the site and discussed the project with the promoter, may well suggest a different approach from the one originally considered. For instance, where the location of the site is particularly important or where the local character must be retained, assessors may feel that a competition limited by region is appropriate. If special skills are required (for instance, an understanding of the fabric of historic buildings), the type of competition which was organised for the renovation of Ashton Court in Bristol or the conversion and extension of Magdalen College, Oxford, might be recommended, where architects with relevant experience are invited to apply for consideration and a shortlist of competitors is selected by the assessors. In other circumstances assessors may feel that a small competition would benefit from being given a wider scope or that a limited competition should be opened up to other practices.

Ideally, no decisions should be completely fixed before the assessors are appointed as they are responsible for ensuring that the competition is properly organised and that the promoter is given advice and assistance to facilitate the successful outcome. It would be within the terms of reference of the assessors, for instance, to inform the promoter if they felt that the site he had selected was inappropriate to the proposed use or if the accommodation required was more than the site could properly be expected to support. Where cost is an important factor, the assessors are also responsible for satisfying themselves, as far as they are able at this stage, that it is possible to fulfil the requirements of the promoter within the cost limits given.

Drawing up the conditions
Once the basis of the competition has been established and the assessors have satisfied themselves that it is viable, their next job is to draw up the conditions.

The conditions fall into four parts: the general conditions, the brief, the instructions to competitors and the site information. In the UK the general conditions follow the wording of the RIBA model form for the particular type of competition and may be drafted by the RIBA Competitions Office for the assessors' approval, but the rest of the information has to be put together by the assessors. For some projects, such as a housing scheme or a primary school for a large authority, there will be a standard brief which cannot be amended to any great extent, even for the purpose of a competition. In other cases, the assessors may have to draw the brief together right from the initial stages. In the Burrell Museum competition, for instance, the assessors arranged for the collection to be put on display and to some extent newly catalogued so that they could determine the areas and the sort of spaces which would be needed. With the help of specialists in museum display, the various bodies involved in financing and promoting the project, and the curator of the collection, they drew up a brief for the competition building.

Even where the promoter has already set out his requirements, the way the brief is presented in the competition conditions is the responsibility of the assessors and it is a responsibility which they take seriously. A number of architects who had acted as assessors on competitions in the UK and abroad were asked what part they had played in drawing up the conditions. Nearly all (95%) said they had been involved in the detailed drawing-up of the brief and the preparation of the conditions and claimed they would not have accepted the appointment had they not been so. Most assessors agree that a good brief should aim to be clear and informative while allowing the designer as much freedom as possible, though attention to costs is liable to be an important consideration in judging the entries.

It is against the criteria established in the brief that the assessors make their selection. They have been involved in the whole process and the priorities which are set out in the brief are the ones they will look for in the entries. If a solution involves contravening any of the mandatory conditions then a competitor, if he wants to stand a chance of winning a competition, should look for an alternative answer within the terms of the brief. A good team of assessors will already have pushed the limits as far as they can to give maximum freedom to the competitor.

Questions and answers
In all RIBA project competitions and in many ideas competitions, competitors are allowed a period after the conditions are issued in which to study the brief and submit questions. These questions are gathered together and put to the assessors, who are required to prepare an explanatory memorandum, based on the questions, to be circulated to all competitors. Assessors find this question period valuable in that it gives all competitors a chance to study the brief and if there are any points which require clarification or any errors or misunderstandings in the conditions, they will be picked up.

In the RIBA system all questions used to be answered individually but it was found that this tended to lead assessors into giving information which inadvertently closed options they preferred to leave open to the competitors. This was changed in the major revision of the system in 1968, although some competitions promoted since that date have continued the old system.

A new system is being tried out in the UK in the Regional Special Category competitions and in certain limited competitions. Instead of the normal question and answer period, competitors are invited to meet the assessors and representatives of the promoter at a "forum" where they can discuss the brief together. Minutes are taken and any technical information is noted and these are circulated to all competitors. As with the explanatory memorandum normally prepared by the assessors, these minutes become part of the official conditions for the competition. The organisers of Regional competitions, which are limited to six or eight firms, are very enthusiastic about the way the experimental forum meetings have worked and the valuable contribution they have made to a closer relationship among all concerned in the competition. It is likely that this system (which is very popular in Germany) will be used more extensively where there is a limited number of competitors but assessors feel that it would not be feasible for large open competitions.

Presentation of entries: instructions to competitors
The RIBA gives guidance on the sort of material which should be required from competitors but it is the responsibility of the assessors to define what is to be submitted and how it is to be presented so that they are able to judge the competition and select the winning scheme on a fair and informative basis.

Assessors claim to be satisfied with the sort of limitations which are imposed by the RIBA regulations at present. They want simple, straightforward drawings, limited in size and number, accompanied by a clear, short report, all submitted in a way which makes handling easy and allows comparisons to be made readily between one scheme and another. Many assessors feel that models can be valuable but stress that they must be simple working models built to a standard set out in the conditions. Assessors are not the ones who encourage expansive presentations and many would be pleased to see the number and scale of drawings limited still further, especially in the first stage of a two-stage competition.

The Competitions Committee are moving towards a more flexible attitude to presentation, but assessors do not seem to see a need for this. The comments they made when questioned can be summed up by the statement "the plainest possible".

Judging
The RIBA does not recommend any particular procedure to be followed by assessors and no pro forma of criteria exists. The regulations state that it is the duty of assessors

"to make their Award in strict accordance with the conditions. The Award should be in the form of a formal statement signed by all the assessors, setting out the number of designs examined and the order of the premiums awarded. The Award should be accompanied by a separate report to the promoter informing him of the quality of the designs submitted, of the merits of the premiated and commended schemes and other schemes of interest and, where necessary, of any modifications which ought to be made to the winning scheme."
(Regulation 7f)

In the notes of guidance, assessors are advised to

"elect a Chairman and get together before they start to establish how they intend to carry out the judging in the most appropriate way for the particular competition".

No pattern is indicated for this, and the procedure to be followed is left entirely to the discretion of the jury of assessors.

Assessors usually work out some process of elimination by which they end up with a shortlist of between 10% and 25% of the schemes. These are then discussed very fully, their merits are debated and they are eventually placed in some order. It is the final stage that assessors find most time-consuming and most difficult. In fact, assessors are often disappointed at the general level of competition entries and say that they find a relatively small percentage which stand any real chance. However, with the sort of entry that competitions get at the moment, a small percentage can mean anything between twenty and fifty schemes, whch is still enough to give a wide range of solutions and make the assessors' task a difficult one.

As there are no rules established for the process of assessing, can any general guidelines be drawn from the way people involved in judging recent competitions have tackled the problem?

"With large competitions each assessor went through the drawings individually, and those where there was unanimity of view for elimination were excluded. The same process was repeated until we got through to about fifty entries; following a major debate a majority view prevailed over elimination. When we were down to about twenty schemes, there was a detailed joint debate on each project to arrive at the final solution either for the second stage or for the winning entries."

"We drew up main criteria to help eliminate. Finally each assessor presented in detail a limited number of schemes to the others, with a recommendation and reasons why any scheme should be eliminated or go through. It put the assessor on the spot."

"We had no pro forma (it would depend on the character of the scheme). The method adopted was
1. preliminary subjective and individual elimination
2. group agreement on preliminary elimination
3. subjective individual selection of long shortlist
4. group agreement on long shortlist
5. group elimination and final group agreement of shortlist."

RIBA guidance notes take up this last point and warn

"a check list of design criteria may be drawn up but assessors should be careful that they are not prejudging the designs by imposing selected solutions which could be irrelevant to a radically different approach to the problem".

The system evolved by most groups of assessors is one of a slow process of elimination, by a mixture of individual assessment and group agreement, subjective and objective criticism with some criteria established at the outset and others evolving with the more detailed consideration of the designs. The emphasis at the beginning is on identifying and discarding those schemes which everybody agrees are not of a sufficiently high standard rather than "picking the winners". Most juries do return to the discarded piles when they are down to their final shortlist to check that they have not thrown out any scheme during the preliminary discussions which should have been included. Sometimes slightly obscure solutions become clearer after the different approaches have been considered in depth. At least one competition winner has been rescued from the reject pile in this way.

Technical assessment
The RIBA regulations, in common with the UIA regulations and those of most other countries, permit assessors to recommend that technical examiners be appointed to assist in the preliminary stages of judging the competition. These people have to be architects and may be assistants in the assessors' own practices or employed by the promoter, provided they are not eligible to enter the competition.

The duties of the technical examiners are strictly limited. They are employed to check that the technical requirements of the brief have been met (i.e. that the necessary accommodation is provided, that the site limits have not been exceeded, etc.) and to report to the assessors on that basis, probably using a pro forma which the assessors have prepared. They take no part in the judging as such and their job is to report, not to select. No entries are disqualified by the technical examiners. There are various ways of organising this work. In a competition where the number of entries is limited, it is likely that the technical examiners will be asked to go through the entries and prepare their reports before the assessors meet but in a large open competition the technical assessment will probably be made alongside that of the assessors, i.e. the technical examiners will be provided with accommodation near where the assessors are meeting and entries will be handed to them during the course of the assessment with requests that various details be checked. This sort of checking work is an integral part of the judging process in any but the most straightforward ideas competition, and assessors find the services of properly appointed technical examiners invaluable.

Specialist advice

Assessors may also ask a promoter to make specialist services available to them. Normally, a quantity surveyor is appointed to advise on cost, both in the preparation of the conditions and in checking selected schemes before a final decision is made either at the end of the first or second stage of a competition. Other experts may be called in where appropriate. As with technical examiners, specialist consultants are not assessors and do not take any part in selecting the winning designs. It is the duty of the assessors to reach a decision on the basis of their own judgement, supported by any specialist advice they feel they need.

Commitment to the promoter

The assessors have a commitment to the profession generally to see that a competition is properly organised and assessed and that the judgement is made on architectural criteria in accordance with the conditions. They also have a commitment to the RIBA to see that the regulations are properly applied and that the integrity of the competitions system is maintained. In addition they have a commitment to the promoter, whose professional advisers they are throughout the whole course of the competition.

Assessors are appointed as a jury and they are asked to aim at reaching a unanimous decision. However, if this is impossible, a simple majority vote is usually acceptable and is binding on all the jury members. Occasionally, assessors who have disagreed with the majority decision have insisted on stating their case but the RIBA feels that this weakens the promoter's position and undermines the authority of the jury and strongly discourages assessors from taking this course.

Once the assessors have reached their decision they are required to submit a report to the promoter summarising the response to the competition and setting out in detail the reasons for their award. This document should also make any necessary criticisms of the winning and premiated schemes and draw attention to any changes which, in the opinion of the assessors, need to be made to the winning design. However, in the interests of the promoter, who has to get approval for the selected scheme before it can be built, assessors are asked to stress the positive qualities of the winning design and draw attention to those aspects which have led to its selection as the winner. This report is a confidential document from the assessors to the promoter. Although it is often made available in its entirety to the competitors and the press, the promoters are under no obligation to do so.

Finally, as soon as the competition envelopes are opened and the name of the winner is known, the assessors have an obligation to satisfy themselves that he has the experience and can develop the resources to carry out the work effectively and to inform the promoter of their recommendation on this point (see Chapter 7).

Only when the winner is appointed (or the competition properly terminated and the commitments honoured) are the duties of the assessors complete. Once an architect is commissioned for the project, the normal client/architect relationship is established and the official work of the assessors is over.

Why take the job on?

Assessing a competition can be a long and sometimes onerous responsibility. The architects who take it on are paid fees in accordance with a published scale which is related to the size of a competition, except in Regional Special Category competitions where they offer their services free. The amount of work involved in assessing a competition is, however, not so directly related to the size of the project, and a prestige job, where a number of people are involved in the decision-making process, can be a very time-consuming business for the assessors, and one in which the financial rewards are not great.

However, it is not difficult to find people who are willing to take on this work, even on the Regional competitions. If architects do turn down an invitation to assess a competition more often than not it is because they feel their practice should not be excluded from submitting an entry. When they do take it on, the reasons they give for accepting the appointment are, on the whole, idealistic.

The actual process of judging the entries for the first or second stage of a competition takes between two and five days, but this can be the culmination of many months (and sometimes years) of work. There are meetings to ascertain the promoter's requirements, draw up conditions, answer the questions, prepare the report, establish the winning architect's capabilities and present the result, so that any fees are usually well earned. Although there must be an element of personal prestige in being named as an assessor for an important national project, few architects would be prepared to take the job on unless they believed the competition to be worthwhile and were interested in the work for its own sake.

10 International competitions

UIA jurisdiction

Where competitions are open to architects or teams led by architects from two or more countries, they fall within the jurisdiction of the International Union of Architects (UIA) whose headquarters are in Paris.

The UIA was set up to unite architects throughout the world on a democratic basis, to represent the profession internationally and to encourage co-operation on activities related to the practice of architecture. Since the Constituent Assembly met in Lausanne in July 1948 to initiate the UIA, membership has grown to include more than seventy countries throughout the world. The UIA was given responsibility for international competitions by UNESCO and the first regulations were adopted at the UNESCO General Conference in New Delhi in 1965. These have recently been revised and the new version is to be put to the UNESCO General Conference in Nairobi in 1976 for approval and ratification. In anticipation of this approval the revised regulations are already being recommended to promoters, and model forms have been drawn up to give guidance. The full text of the revised *Regulations for International Competitions in Architecture and Town Planning* is given in the appendices to this book.

In most countries the architectural associations endorse the UIA jurisdiction over competitions in principle at least, and undertake to instruct their members not to enter competitions which do not have UIA approval. This agreement is fully endorsed by the RIBA, and members who enter "banned" or non-approved competitions may find themselves charged with contravening the Code of Professional Conduct.

As with UK competitions, governments and other organisations can bypass the regulations by inviting specific architects to submit designs on a fee basis or by inviting developers to submit designs with a bid for the project on a package deal basis. In the latter case it is assumed that the architect who prepares the design is employed by the developer and remunerated in the normal way. Where UK architects submit designs in return for a fee, this should be calculated on the basis of the amount of work required and should be in accordance with scale fees as set out in the RIBA Conditions of Engagement. With these exceptions, all competitive work at an international level should be undertaken by RIBA members, only if it is within the terms of a UIA-approved competition.

An outline of the system
The competition system has a long history in many countries and the basic principles, which are well established, do not vary greatly. The UIA regulations, in common with those of most member countries, provide for ideas or project competitions, or a mixture of the two, require anonymity amongst competitors, establish a named jury and provide some safeguards for the architect in the use of the winning designs. In addition to the normal clauses defining the aspects listed above, the UIA regulations require that the competition documents be published in one of the official languages of the UIA — i.e. in English, French, Spanish or Russian — or be accompanied by a translation in one of these languages. The jury has to be international, "composed of the smallest reasonable number of persons of different nationality, and in any event should be an odd number and should not exceed seven. The majority of them are to be architects." Competitors are required to submit their entries in the official language of the competition but international competitions are frequently conducted in more than one official language and it is unusual to find a competition in which neither English nor French is permitted.

Submitting an entry
International competitions are costly, both for the promoter and the competitor. They are usually for prestige projects (such as the Paris Arts Centre, the UN headquarters building in Vienna and the Sofia Opera House), for large-scale developments (such as the competition for a new town at Vilamoura in the Algarve, Portugal) or for a major urban redevelopment (for instance, downtown Santiago or the Tertiary Centre in Dunkirk). As a great deal of background information has to be given and sent to all competitors, registration fees tend to be high compared with RIBA competitions: £20 to £50 is not unusual. The UIA regulations state that "where a deposit is required for the competition conditions, unless otherwise stated, this deposit shall be returned to competitors who submit a bona fide design", which means that a deposit may be regarded as an entry fee and in that case will not be returned to competitors who decide not to compete and want to send back the conditions. However, most

78

promoters publish an outline programme to give intending competitors some idea of what is involved. The RIBA Library should also have a set of conditions for all UIA competitions for members' reference, but this cannot be guaranteed as some promoters are loath to send out complimentary copies.

The main expense, in addition to the hours spent working out the design, is preparing the submission and getting it to the promoter. International competitions often require a model to be submitted, especially in the second stage. Both drawings and models have to have customs clearance and although the UIA suggests to promoters that they make prior arrangements with the customs authorities to ensure speedy clearance of projects, it is advisable, particularly in the case of models, to check on the dispatch arrangements well in advance of the closing date and to employ an agent or arrange a contact in the port of arrival to see that the packages are cleared and forwarded to the promoter. Because of the anonymity requirement, it can be difficult for the promoter to inform a competitor if part of his entry has gone astray.

In addition to the freight charges, competitors may find themselves involved in fees for translating documents. A professional technical translator charges a minimum of £15 per thousand words, depending on the technical difficulty and the language used. The Institute of Linguists publishes a scale of charges and is also able to put people in touch with appropriate translators. As far as scale and dimensions are concerned, there are no longer any problems, as the metric scale is now universal in the architectural world.

Possible difficulties

The UIA has recently drawn up model forms of conditions and instructions to promoters to facilitate the proper organisation of competitions and has set up a system of regional co-ordinators to be responsible for competitions in their particular area of the world. However, controlling competitions at an international level is difficult, and political pressures can influence the conduct of a competition, even if the conditions are in order and the UIA approval has been sought and obtained. The story of the 1970 Vienna competition which Building Design Partnership came so near to winning but lost in an unscheduled second stage illustrates the power game that a practice can find itself in when competing for projects of this importance. The UIA approval does safeguard the interests of the competitor to a considerable extent and if things do go wrong, the individual has an internationally recognised organisation to take up the case on his behalf. But it is difficult to safeguard a competitor in every situation, so it is inadvisable for an individual or small practice to put resources which they cannot afford into an international competition, even when an honorarium is supposedly guaranteed.

On the subject of prize money, in some countries (mostly in the Eastern bloc) there are currency regulations which prohibit a prizewinner from taking his money out of the country. Other countries may place a tax on the prize money so that the competitor actually receives considerably less than the amount stated, but the UIA regulations do require that where this is the case it be set out in the conditions. Most of the difficulties in international competitions arise from the problems of dispatching the documents. Promoters do not always take the trouble to check on the postal requirements of different countries or on the amount of time taken in transit. This can mean that a timetable which looks reasonable on the programme becomes very tight for overseas competitors because they have had to wait so long for the information. Promoters can also be rather less than scrupulous in providing adequate translations of the documents, knowing that they are safeguarded, were a dispute to arise, by the fact that the version in the original language would be regarded as the official one.

The future of international competitions

In his preface to the 1973/4 *Review of International Competitions*, Michel Weill, the Secretary General of the UIA, expressed his concern over the huge number of entries which open competitions were attracting and looked to regional competitions, limited to architects in a particular area, to solve the problem. This is in line with the current regionalisation policy of the UIA, decided upon by the Assembly at Varna in 1972 when four statutory regions were created. These were: Western Europe; Eastern Europe and the near East; America; Africa, Asia and Australia. (In June 1975, the African countries were made into a separate group, group five.)

Most architects will appreciate Michel Weill's concern that international competitions be limited to some extent. Total entries of over 500 schemes, which some of the more important competitions, such as the one for the design of Amsterdam City Hall, have been attracting in recent years, obviously pose problems which are more than the promoters or the assessors can cope with. Not everybody, however, would agree that the system of regional competitions which he proposes, cutting across long-established links and separating countries with similar cultural backgrounds, is the best solution. Open

The design and the building

Illustrations 1–5 show drawings of competition-winning entries and photographs of the buildings they subsequently produced.

1 a, b St Paul's Cathedral Choir School, London: an example of a winning design in a limited competition. *Architects*: Architects' Co-Partnership. *RIBA Architecture Award 1968.*

2 a, b, c Lillington Gardens, Pimlico, London SW1: phase 1. *Architects:* Darbourne and Darke. *RIBA Architecture Award 1970.*

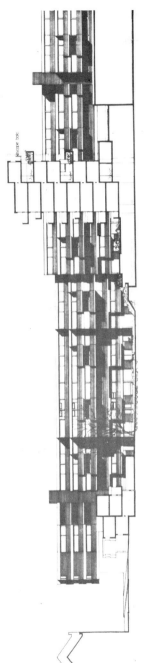

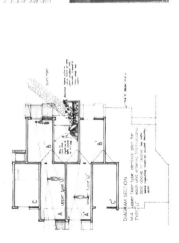

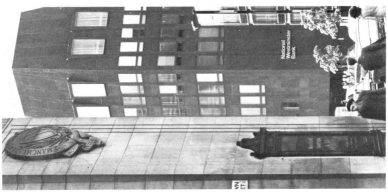

3 a, b Manchester District Bank, Manchester: an example of a winning design in a limited competition. *Architects*: Casson Conder and Partners. *RIBA Architecture Award 1971.*

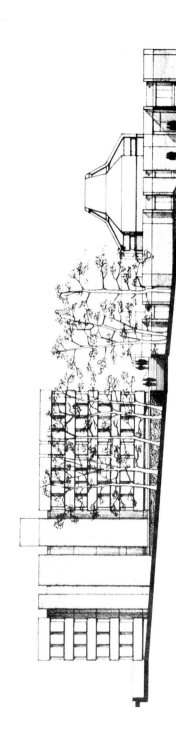

4 a, b Antrim County Hall, Ballymena, Northern Ireland: an example of a winning design in an open competition. *Architects*: Burman and Goodal. *RIBA Architecture Award 1971.*

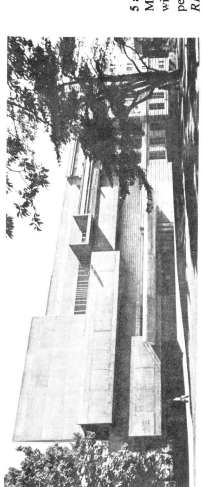

5 a, b Extension to the Ulster Museum, Belfast: an example of a winning design in an open competition. *Architect*: Francis Pym. *RIBA Architecture Award 1972.*

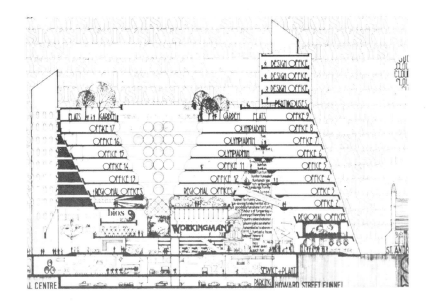

Methods of presentation: illustrations

6 Illustration from the report submitted for the River Clyde study and ideas competition by a team from Strathclyde University (third-prizewinners).

7 Collage by Volker Stöcks illustrating his prizewinning design in an ideas competition for a jeweller's shop in the year 2000.

8 Part of a drawing, "View to Ride", showing the effect of siting the building close to trees, in Barry Gasson and John Meunier's prizewinning design for the Burrell Museum competition.

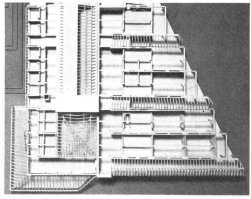

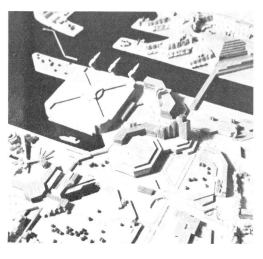

Methods of presentation: models

9 Model of Casson Conder and Partners' winning design for the limited competition for new civic halls in Derby.
10 Model by Gasson and Meunier for the second stage of the Burrell Museum competition.
11 Part of the model of Renton Howard Wood Levin's winning entry for the River Clyde study and ideas competition.

Methods of presentation: photographs of models

12 Eric Lyons's prizewinning design in an international competition for a tourist development at Vilamoura, Portugal.

13 Jeremy and Fenella Dixon's winning entry for the Northampton County Hall competition.

14 Photomontage of the model of Spence and Webster's winning design in the Commonwealth competition for the New Parliamentary Building in London.

competitions, involving some preliminary selection, either by the assessors or the national sections, might be a more acceptable answer. Promoters want to choose from a range of people with the right design skills and experience rather than from within limited geographical boundaries, and many architects would certainly object if, for instance, they saw the UIA directing the rich oil states to limit their competitions to 'Eastern Europe and the near East'.

The size of entry is not the only problem. Recently there have been a number of major competitions which have not had UIA approval, partly because the UIA has not made sufficient efforts to draw the attention of would-be promoters to its regulations. Architects who are members of associations whose codes of conduct require them to observe UIA jurisdiction are worried by the number of non-approved competitions which have gone ahead and attracted entries. A working group was set up at the end of 1975 with members drawn from national sections with experience of organising competitions, to plan a course of action for publicising and promoting the UIA competition system. It is likely that future international competitions will be placed into one of three categories:

1. competitions which are organised in consultation with the UIA and are in line with its regulations. National sections will be recommended to encourage their members to enter
2. competitions which have been organised without UIA consultation and do not follow the regulations in all respects, but are run on a generally acceptable basis. The UIA will point out any possible difficulties and leave it to the national sections to decide whether or not their members should enter
3. competitions which are unacceptable, in that they contravene basic principles. The UIA will ask national sections to instruct their members not to enter.

Such a system would give the UIA and its national sections more flexibility in dealing with competitions. At the same time it is likely that the working group would decide to pursue a far more active promotional campaign pointing out the advantages of promoting a properly organised and approved competition (category 1).

Is it worth entering for international competitions?
Over the past ten years there have been, on average, four or five international competitions each year for a variety of projects, and, in addition, one or two ideas competitions.

The prestige of the buildings which have been commissioned in this way is considerably greater than the actual money value of the projects would suggest. International competitions also play a valuable role in bringing together architectural expertise, allowing architects from one country to assess their own standpoint and compare their approach with that of architects from very different cultural and economic backgrounds: Equally valuable is the opportunity afforded to the members of the juries to establish links through their meetings and these can last well beyond the period of the competition.

Documentation
Regulations for International Competitions in Architecture and Town Planning, reproduced in Appendix C
International Union of Architects *Review of International Competitions*. This appeared for the first time in 1974 covering the years 1973-74. It will be a regular publication provided the number of competitions justifies its production

11 Competitions in Europe

As explained in the previous chapter, UIA regulations are valid wherever architects from more than one country are involved in a competition. The UIA does, however, recognise the validity of certain historic, cultural or economic links and in addition to international competitions there may also be competitions open to architects from groups of countries — e.g. Scandinavia, the Eastern bloc or the Commonwealth — which are run in accordance with regulations sanctioned by all member countries of the particular group concerned. The European Economic Community would be an acceptable unit for organising competitions but as yet no regulations exist nor are any planned. One competition was organised by the EEC for a building for its own use, but this was run in accordance with the UIA regulations.

In most European competition systems, competitors may be associated with people who are not eligible to enter in their own right. British architects could, therefore, enter the national competitions of other countries, provided they did so in association with an architect who fulfilled the entry requirements. In fact, some American practices took on Canadian architects in order to enter the Commonwealth competition for the New Parliamentary Building, and although this was not within the spirit of the competition, it was impossible to render them ineligible.

Basically, most architectural competition systems are similar to that of the RIBA, but a point to watch most carefully for differences is the promoter's rights over and commitment to the winning designs. In many European countries the winner is not automatically appointed or paid compensation and the promoter may have certain rights with regard to the prizewinning schemes which would not be within the British law of copyright. However, to compensate, the prizes are often considerably higher than in this country.

It is possible to divide Europe into two as far as use of the competition system is concerned. There is a group of countries which have a thriving competition system. These are the Scandinavian countries — Norway, Sweden, Denmark and Finland — and the

German-speaking countries — Germany, Switzerland and to a lesser extent Austria. The rest of Europe has very few competitions although in the United Kingdom and France there are moves to get the system more widely used and authorities in Ireland also seem to be interested in encouraging more competitions. Countries which have no strong tradition of internal competitions such as Italy and Portugal have been the source of many of the recent international competitions, which may be a sign that they, too, are beginning to take an interest in this way of finding a solution to architectural problems.

Germany
The country in which the competitions are most widely used is Germany, which has between 200 and 400 every year. By way of comparison, in the whole of the UK there are between five and ten competitions each year and even in the "good old days" before the Second World War, a total of forty marked an exceptional year. The competition system in Germany is an interesting study which suggests that there is considerably more to organising competitions than setting up a good system. Germany is a federal state, with strong regional characteristics, and the way the competition system is used varies greatly from one area to another, although the competition regulations are drawn up centrally by the Bund Deutscher Architekten (BDA) and agreed upon by representatives of the organisations who use the system, the German Association of Communes (Deutschen Städtetag). Each of the eleven Länder, or districts, of Germany appoints its own competitions committee to be responsible for developing the system within its own area and most competitions are organised on this regional basis, with the number of competitions varying enormously from one Land to another. For instance, in 1969 there were 365 competitions in the whole of Germany of which seventy-three were promoted in Nordrhein-Westfalen compared with only one in the Bremen, Hamburg area.

The BDA, the central organisation for the competition system, is an association of private architects and consists mainly of partners. The majority of salaried architects in private practice and in public authorities belong, not to the BDA, but to one of the Chambers of Architects which are organised on a Land basis. The BDA therefore forms a strong pressure group which acts in the interest of the principals in private practice and sees competitions as a vital method of getting work financed by public funds into private offices. Practices tend to be small in Germany, consisting of a studio of a small core of architects. For large projects more assistants are drawn

84

in and then allowed to disperse once the job is complete. For example, the scheme for the Munich Olympics was the result of a competition which was won by Behnisch and Partners, a group of six architects, split between Munich and Stuttgart. To get the scheme off the ground the team grew to over seventy and once the project was completed the practice reversed to more or less its original form. A competition system as widely used as in Germany means that practices must have a fluid and versatile approach as few practices can be sure of maintaining a regular supply of large projects to keep a permanent large staff of architects.

The system by which competitions are organised is very similar to that run by the RIBA with one major exception. In open competitions the promoter is not committed to building the winning design but only to declaring his intention to commission the author of one of the premiated or purchased schemes to develop the entry, if one is found which presents a suitable solution to the problem and the competitor is capable of carrying it out (c.f. The RIBA's recently introduced Promoter Choice competition). "Purchases" are made in addition to awards and are used to commend schemes and buy certain limited rights of implementation for the promoter. The regulations do not allow prizes to be given to schemes which do not comply with the competition conditions but they do allow purchases to be made. It would be possible, therefore, under the German system, for the promoter to commission an architect who had ignored the conditions if he thought the scheme was what he wanted. The fact that the majority of winning schemes do get built is due, not to the regulations, but to the dedication of the regional committees who see it as one of their duties to explain the scheme to the promoter and lobby for its implementation. In spite of the competition system being organised centrally by the private-practice-orientated BDA, the Chambers of Architects in some regions actively support the system and encourage its use.

The open competition accounts for only half of the project competitions; the rest are limited by invitation. Once a practice has won an open competition it stands a good chance of being invited to take part in limited competitions for similar projects. A new practice is therefore given the opportunity to build up its workload through the competition system. Some practices get their work more or less exclusively in this way and allow for about 10% of the capacity of the office to be set aside to preparing competition entries. In limited competitions the prizewinner is guaranteed an appointment but not necessarily for the whole job. He may be asked to develop his designs to tender stage, when the more detailed work and supervision of the building work is taken over by the promoter's architects.

Two-stage competitions are very rare in Germany and when they do occur they are organised in two distinct sections: an ideas competition followed by a limited competition with prizes awarded at the end of each part.

Whether the competition system will continue to be so widely used is doubtful and the BDA is worried that more work will be taken over by the local authorities and the package dealers. Large cities such as Stuttgart and Munich have their own architectural departments which undertake much of the design work for projects within the conurbation. But individual small towns and communities have retained responsibility for many publicly financed buildings such as schools and, although funded by large regional authorities, the design and construction are the responsibility of the local community. It is at this level that the competition system flourishes.

Because of the wide use of competitions, the technical press in Germany is able to produce two monthly magazines devoted entirely to competition designs: *Architekturwettbewerbe* and *Bauwelt*. These provide a valuable source of information on a wide range of projects from individual buildings to redevelopment plans for whole areas. Reference copies are available in the RIBA Library.

*Switzerland**
Switzerland is second to Germany in the number of competitions held each year — between seventy and one hundred. When you consider the size of the country and its population, this number represents a significant proportion of the profession's work. Nearly all of these are promoted by public authorities. There is no legal requirement that public buildings should be the subject of competitions but many of them are.

Architectural competitions in Switzerland are governed by regulations laid down by the Schweizerischer Ingenieur und Architekten Verein in their document 152. This covers eligibility, composition of the jury, documentation, judging, guidelines for assessors, amount of prize money and number of prizes.

Apart from volume, competitions differ most from those organised in the UK on the question of eligibility. Competitions can be open, but are often restricted to canton or parish or even by religious belief. This

*This section is based on an article "Competitions in Switzerland" by Cedric Ellis, which appeared in *Architectural Competitions News,* Number 5, 1975.

has the effect that in normal times and in normal conditions, entries would be no more than about fifty. The average standard of entry is very high because architects all see competitions as a way of winning valuable commissions for their practice and because, with more competitions to choose from, they can be more selective. (This aspect of regarding competitions as a normal way of getting work is reflected by a clause in the regulations which states that employees may enter a competition only if their boss is not competing.)

Under the Swiss system an architect is appointed to act as professional adviser to the promoter; his duties include clarifying the brief, drawing up the conditions and undertaking much of the work which is the responsibility of the assessors in the RIBA system. The jury is appointed to judge the entries and select the winning schemes. The size of the jury for any competition depends on the size and complexity of the project. The jury is composed of architects (sometimes including other specialists concerned with the particular building type) and lay members who are largely local government or political figures (who will be responsible for progressing the scheme), as well as people who will be responsible for management of the completed building. In Swiss practice there is always one more architect (or member of the professional group) then lay juror and it is very rare that this is not found to be satisfactory. This is because juries rarely split on a professional/lay basis and architects are not always unanimous in their choice.

The prize fund in Swiss competitions is made up of a number of prizes and "purchases". Although all prizewinning schemes become the property of the promoter, they may be used only for the building and site which was the subject of the competition. Like many European systems, the Swiss one allows the architectural merit of the submissions to be established but leaves the promoter free to build one of the other prizewinning designs if he prefers it to that awarded first prize. (When calculating the amount of prize money to be offered, Swiss regulations require promoters to take into account not only the estimated value of the project but to include a "difficulty quotient" which varies with the complexity of the problem.) A large percentage of the competition-winning schemes are built.

Recent proposals in Aargau have been aimed at strengthening the competition system. In order to reduce costs, it is proposed that fewer drawings to a smaller scale be asked for and that in some circumstances elevations not be required. There are some doubts as to whether a competition can be judged on this basis, but the decision on the documents required still rests with the jury for any particular project. Because there is some concern about the appointment of a young and inexperienced winner, it has been suggested that in such cases the architect be appointed only for the sketch proposals and development of the design to a point after which he must collaborate with a more experienced colleague to carry out the scheme. On a more complicated project, this collaboration could be required from the outset. It has also been suggested that in order to have even more support for the winning scheme, a larger number of lay people attend the judging process, but without voting rights. Clearly this could present problems unless there was a specific undertaking to abide by the decision of the jury.

Generally the promoters and the public are happy with the results of competitions and this is obviously helped by the fact that the public is called on to ratify the scheme at various stages, including the financing of the project and the budget and the final instruction to build.

Scandinavia: Sweden, Norway, Denmark, Finland and Iceland
The Scandinavian countries are often cited as having a very large number of competitions but, in fact, in each of them there are on average between ten and fifteen competitions a year, with a further two or three which are open to the whole of Scandinavia.* These include town planning competitions, as the two professions form part of the same organisations. However, if you compare the number of competitions in these countries with the UK or the USA on the basis of size of the profession rather than a direct number ratio, you can understand why the competition system has more impact there. In Finland, for instance, the SAFA (Suomen Arkkitehtiliitto Finlands Arkitekförbund) has under 1,000 members. In 1973 there were ten open competitions and four limited competitions, and one out of every two architects submitted an entry. Proportionally, this is equivalent to there being at least 180 open competitions and seventy limited competitions in the United Kingdom. Similarly Norway has about 1,000 architects involved in ten to fifteen competitions.

In Norway the system is helped by a Code of Professional Conduct which forbids members of the institute to compete with each other on the same project except in a competitive situation, even with the payment of full scale fees, although there is considerable pressure to

*This average was based on figures for the years 1969 to 1972. Since then there has been a definite decline in the number of competitions in Sweden (only one during the first half of 1975) and in Norway, although the system continues to be well used in Denmark and Finland.

change this. The competition system is also more widely used because the main responsibility of local authority architects' departments is the inspection of plans to see that they conform with building regulations, instead of original design work. There are very few large firms of architects in Norway (only twenty offices employ more than ten architects), so important projects tend to be the subject of competitions. Working against this is the fact that no cost limit is set in competitions and recently clients have been put off by the high cost of carrying out competition designs.

The Scandinavian system is very similar to the German one except that two-stage competitions are recommended for most projects. The promoter is normally only required to commission the author of one of the winning or purchased schemes to carry out further studies and, again, he may purchase an entry which contravenes the binding conditions and select it for development. In Finland the regulations allow any Finnish citizen to enter a competition and the option exists in other Scandinavian countries for a competition to be opened to the general public. In practice, they are normally entered and won by architects.

France

A competition system exists in France, similar to that of the other European countries mentioned, and is administered by the Conseil de l'Ordre Supérieure des Architectes. There are very few competitions (a total of fifty-six in the ten years from 1962 to 1972) and according to a government report prepared by the Ministère des Affaires Culturelles et de l'Environnement many of them were badly organised and ignored the regulations. A number of past competitions produced such national monuments as the colonnade of the Louvre, the French Academy, the Carrousel Arch and the Opéra, but the system has fallen into disrepute. "Competitions are often the object of dishonest manoeuvres", states the report. "People organise them to get a bit of publicity, but refuse to take the responsibility for the outcome — the temptation to play the sorcerer's apprentice is great". Central government, new towns and local authorities have been responsible for the recent bad image of competitions, as 96% of those promoted in the last ten years have been in the public sector.

The regulations require that juries should be limited in size and that architects should be in the majority, but this rule is often disregarded. For example, in one recent competition there was a jury of twenty-six people, of whom eighteen were part of the promoter's administrative organisation, four represented central government and the remaining four only were independent architects. In a fifth of the competitions the jury were not named at all and in a third they were identified only by position. Information is sent out late and there is a suspicion that juries are often influenced by outside organisations such as developers. There is a commitment to appoint the architect responsible for the winning design but this, too, is seldom recognised.

On the other hand, international competitions promoted by French authorities do have to adhere to the UIA regulations if they are to be given approval and as the UIA has its headquarters in Paris, it is able to exercise some influence here. Recent international competitions promoted by French organisations, such as the ideas competitions for the development of part of Dunkirk and the competition for the Plateau Beaubourg Centre in Paris, have been very well organised. The problem the UIA faces is illustrated by the fact that three international competitions launched by French promoters were banned by the UIA in 1974 alone.

The report cited previously shows that the French government is very much aware of the problem and is interested in encouraging a properly organised competition system as a way of giving work to young architects, opening up research channels, improving the quality of architecture and interesting the public in the built environment. It sets a target of 250 competitions a year, with an average project value of £1.5m. This apparently represents 4.6% of publicly financed building, and calculating the additional cost of holding a competition as 1%, the surcharge on the state for this number of competitions would be .038% of the total construction budget.

Italy

In Italy there are very few competitions as public authorities tend to prefer the package deal. The Turin Association of Architects has undertaken a study to encourage the further use of the system but this has not yet resulted in any positive outcome.

Ireland

Competition regulations are issued by the Royal Institute of the Architects of Ireland and are similar to, though less strictly defined than, those issued by the RIBA. Irish competitions are, in principle, open to architects who are resident or were born in Ireland and are members of the RIAI or are eligible to become members of that body.

Irish competitions are not very frequent, but they are covered by the British technical press.

A variation of the standard ideas competition has recently been introduced and used twice with success. The first was for a secondary school, designed to the standard brief, issued by the Department of Education, and the second was for housing within conservation areas of Dublin. In both these cases the promoters wanted to build up a pool of architects who could be commissioned for similar jobs. Each competition could, therefore, have resulted in commissions for all the prizewinning competitors.

Working in Europe
Negotiations are proceeding on the mutual recognition of qualifications and free movement of architects within the countries of the EEC, but progress is slow and has been made more so by the expansion of the EEC from six to nine countries. The UK delegation of the Liaison Committee of Architects in the Common Market (LCACM) is trying to speed up the process and, to some extent, anticipate the agreement. A number of firms are now working in Europe in partnership or association with local architects and for this no formal mutual recognition or registration is necessary. The LCACM has agreed in principle that a more systematic extension of such arrangements is desirable and the RIBA is hoping to work out machinery, involving the Clients' Advisory Service, to help architects form these links. At the present time, this is the only way that British architects can enter competitions in Europe.

To provide information on architectural practice in each of the European Economic Community countries, the RIBA and ARCUK have published a series of guides, details of the code of conduct, conditions of engagement, model forms of contract, etc., in both English and the original language. These are obtainable from RIBA Publications, 66 Portland Place, London W1.

12 Competitions in the Commonwealth

Outside the few European countries mentioned in the previous chapter, there is a general dearth of competitions. The whole of the Commonwealth outside the UK can muster only about five competitions a year. But where there are competitions they still attract interest. For instance, the one major international competition in 1975 was organised from Canada to coincide with the Vancouver Conference on the human habitat. It asked for low-cost solutions to the problems of housing large numbers in the rapidly growing urban settlements in the developing countries. There were over 2,000 requests for the conditions — enough interest to support twenty such competitions. Looking through recent international competitions it can be seen that Commonwealth architects respond to competition opportunities as much as architects throughout the rest of the world. In the Amsterdam City Hall competition, for instance, 5% of the entries came from Canada. On the few occasions when UK competitions have been open to architects throughout the Commonwealth (such as the competition for the New Parliamentary Building), up to a third of the entries have come from overseas in spite of the difficulties of visiting the site and the expense of sending in the designs.

The RIBA has never exercised any form of control over architectural competitions in Australia, New Zealand, Canada or South Africa, which have their own regulations and competition systems. However, until 1958 all architectural competitions in other countries in the Commonwealth came under the jurisdiction of the RIBA. The names of the assessors had to be put forward or approved by the President of the RIBA and the draft conditions sent for approval.

Just over ten years ago the Commonwealth Association of Architects was formed and its membership grew as the smaller countries gained independence. The RIBA regulations continued to be recommended as the basis for all competitions where Commonwealth societies had not already established their own rules. At the beginning of 1975, the CAA decided to introduce its own competition regulations, which were to be based on those issued by the Royal Australian Institute of Architects, as these had been most recently revised (1974). However, as the RAIA regulations were themselves based on the RIBA regulations and followed them in all major respects, the position continues more or less unchanged. It does mean, though, that the Commonwealth Association of Architects may develop the system along different lines in the future.

Some countries are showing an interest in the new types of competition recently introduced by the RIBA. The Bermuda Society of Architects has, for instance, expressed an interest in adapting the Regional Special Category competition to its own particular needs. It is very unlikely that the Commonwealth Association of Architects would object to such alternatives being used.

A few competitions in the last two decades have been open to architects throughout the Commonwealth: Liverpool Cathedral; Lillington Street Housing, promoted by the Westminster City Council; University of Liverpool halls of residence; Paisley and Renfrew municipal buildings; and, more recently, the competition for the extension to the British Houses of Parliament. Apart from one competition (for a hospital in Kuala Lumpur), all the open Commonwealth competitions have been initiated by promoters in the United Kingdom, although other Commonwealth countries have held fully international competitions. There was also a limited competition for a bell tower in Canberra in which three young British practices were invited to compete with three young Australian practices (an Australian practice won), but this is the only one of its type to be held to date.

Australia

Like other Commonwealth countries, Australia has very few competitions (only one or two a year). There are rumours of some major projects possibly being scheduled to go out to competition but nothing has been announced officially.

The RAIA regulations

The *Regulations for the Promotion and Conduct of Competitions*, issued by the Royal Australian Institute of Architects in August 1974, set out the revised rules of the competition system. It is a system similar in all major respects to that of the RIBA (i.e. the basic RIBA system without the more recent variations), so that Chapter 2 on how the RIBA system works can be read for a description of competitions in Australia. The only important difference is that there is a slight variation in the costs of prizes, assessors' fees, etc. The RAIA are aware of the new opportunities which have taken place in the RIBA system and there is no reason why they should not incorporate some of the alternatives into their competitions, should the need arise.

Australian competitions have won fame by producing what is probably the most controversial competition-winning building of the century — the Sydney Opera House (the result, in fact, of an open international competition). In its handout on the competition system the RAIA comments on this design:

"This building would have emerged only as the result of the competition system. Despite its cost and gestation difficulties, it will be one of the great buildings of the twentieth century. One lesson learnt from this competition is that the promoter must have a clear idea of his requirements before the competition is launched. The competition system does not necessarily result in an expensive building."

In the short term the RAIA see the Sydney Opera House saga as detrimental to the more extensive use of the competition system there, but with their newly revised regulations, they may well be able to overcome the misgivings of would-be promoters.

Canada
Canada, like Australia, has a little-used competition system but is taking the trouble to keep it up to date. The most recent revisions undertaken by the Ontario Association of Architects acting on behalf of the Royal Architectural Institute of Canada, were officially approved in April 1975. Each of the nine component associations of the RAIC has autonomous control over registration and practice within its provincial boundaries and had to give approval to the document before it could be published. The Ontario Association of Architects, having now completed the revision of the regulations, is going on to review the competition situation and look at how the system could be more widely used. At the time of writing, this work was very much in its early stages and no suggestions or recommendations had been made.

How the RAIC system works
The RAIC regulations define a competition as follows:

"An architectural competition occurs when two or more architects

and an RAIC member can compete with another only under conditions defined by the Code for the Conduct of Architectural Competitions. This definition seems rather tighter than that of the RIBA which permits competitive work if done for full scale fees but there is a clause in the Canadian regulations allowing "Private Competitions", which are excluded from the requirement to follow the code, provided the architects are paid a fee in accordance with the standard fee schedule.

The Canadian system offers three basic objectives for a competition:

> *"a) Selection of a design work which is intended to be carried out*
> *b) Selection of an architect*
> *c) Selection of a design intended to explore the possibilities of specific types of buildings, materials, construction methods, or intended for research".*

These divisions are roughly comparative with (a) the RIBA's project competitions, (b) Preliminary Project or Promoter Choice competitions and (c) ideas competitions, though the RIAC does not draw the distinction between ideas and project competitions in the same way as the RIBA. The RAIC ideas competition can be held for specific buildings (where there is an intention to go ahead with the work), concentrating on the preliminary design stage, in which the submission requirements are minimal. The promoter is free to conclude the competition at the beginning of the first stage (on payment of the premiums) or to proceed to the second stage to develop the scheme more fully.

As in RIBA competitions there is a commitment by the promoter to appoint the winner as architect for the work, where the outcome of a competition is a design for a specific project. (In the case of the two-stage competition described above, this would come into force only if the promoter decided to proceed to the second stage.) The winner is given an advance of 10% of the total fees due (based on an estimated project value) as his first prize. This is merged with his fees if the job proceeds but if the job or the winning architect is abandoned, then a sum equivalent to a total of 20% of the fees due must be paid in compensation.

The professional adviser
The main difference between RIBA and RAIC competitions is the way

in which they are administered. In common with countries such as the USA and Switzerland, the Canadian system employs the services of a professional adviser, an architect appointed by the promoter to organise a competition on his behalf. (This difference affects the position and obligations of the promoter and assessors far more than the work of the competitors.) It is the job of the professional adviser to get approval for the competition from the appropriate organisation (i.e. the RAIC in the case of an open national competition, or one of the nine component associations for a Regional competition); to advise on the appointment of assessors; to draw up the competition conditions in accordance with the Code; to advise the promoter on the question of overall costs; in the case of a limited competition, to advise on the choice of competitors; to obtain approval for the conditions from the relevant association; to publicise the competition and circulate the conditions; to establish the eligibility of the registered competitors; to answer questions; to examine the designs to see that they conform with the mandatory requirements; to instruct and supervise the assessors (the professional adviser normally acts as chairman of the board of assessors and has a vote); to advise the promoter, competitors and publicity media on the results of the competition; and finally to return registration fees to competitors. In all this he has an assistant with a watching brief on the organisation of the competition. In effect, the professional adviser undertakes most of the work that is done by the RIBA, the promoter and the assessors in the RIBA competition system. He is paid normal scale fees on a per diem basis for the work he does and the competition expenses are paid by the promoter.

Assessors are appointed to judge the competition and select the winning design. They are consulted on the conditions but do not play the important role in drawing them up that they are given in the RIBA system. The board of assessors can include up to nine persons, with architects generally making up one third of the total. It is suggested in the Code that the board should "reflect the character of the general community" and should be composed in the following proportions:

"two professional engineers, representing specialities appropriate to the competition, three architects and four non-architects/non-engineers, representing the general and particular community at large".

In writing the brief, the professional adviser is asked to make a "statement of intent" to identify areas of the program (the conditions) which are considered particularly important and to describe the nature of the solution particularly favoured by the promoter. However it is not to "preclude the possibility of other views being made the basis of a solution".

Entry requirements
Little guidance is given on the nature of the material to be submitted, but in the paper *Guide for Professional Advisers* it is suggested that

> *"Standards of presentation required should be kept to a minimum. Perspectives should be limited in size and number and executed in black and white. White prints mounted on board and lettered with freehand script should suffice. If more elaborate drawings are required for publicity purposes, arrangements for their production may be made at a later date. If a model is required it should be in simple block form."*

(This is taken from the 1969 notes because the revised version, scheduled to accompany the 1975 revision of the Code, was not available at the time of writing. The excerpts from the Code are, however, taken from the 1975 revision which was available in its final draft form.)

Organising a competition through a professional adviser means that a lot of the work is taken off the promoter and placed on the individual architect, who has complete responsibilty for seeing that the competition is satisfactorily completed. However, it does add to the expense of promoting a competition, which is already high in the Canadian system, with reasonably generous prize money and assessors' fees (although these, on a per diem basis, may well be less than in countries where the assessors are responsible for the whole conduct of the competition).

More worrying than the cost aspects is the lack of continuity the system implies in a situation where there are very few competitions (in Ontario, for instance, there has not been a single competition of any type for two years). This must mean that either the same people are asked to take on the job time and time again or that this very responsible position is given to someone who has very little experience of what is involved. A similar system is used in Switzerland, but, with over a hundred competitions a year, these problems do not arise.

New Zealand
To quote the Secretary of the New Zealand Institute of Architects,

98

"competitions here are organised at the whim of the particular client and, at the moment, we do not have any in progress". There are very few competitions in New Zealand, although the New Zealand Institute of Architects has regulations for competitions and takes a positive attitude towards them.

"A method of selection encouraged by the New Zealand Institute of Architects, where the work offers sufficient scope, is by competition....

A client can invite as many architects as he likes to prepare sketch designs, but he must pay each architect the minimum fee of around 1 ½ % of the estimated cost of the building.

As an alternative, architects are allowed to compete against each other in open architectural competitions, held under NAIZ regulations. Architects who take part are prepared to compete without a fee."

The New Zealand competition system is very similar to that of the RIBA in terms of types of competition, eligibility, assessment and appointment of the winning architect. It differs mainly in the way it is organised (as in Canada by a professional adviser) and the distribution of prize money.

"In all cases the first step is the appointment in consultation with the President of the Institute, of a professional adviser, who acts first as a professional consultant and secondly to advise on the type of competition to be held. He will investigate the promoter's requirements in much the same way as if he were the architect commissioned to do the job. In consultation with the promoters he will draw up a clear architectural programme which will form the basis for the printed competition conditions. The second step is the early appointment of the jury of assessors. The professional adviser will be the Chairman of the jury, and most of the other members will be architects of an acknowledged standard. The jury can also include a layman or laymen nominated by the promoter to contribute valuable non-technical skills to the complete process of preparing the brief and selecting the winning design. For a small project, a single architect assessor might be sufficient. All assessors must be nominated by the President of the Institute or approved by him. Assessors receive fees in accordance with a scale set out in the regulations.

"Competition conditions approved as complying with the NZIA

regulations are printed, published and advertised and copies issued to competitors (by the promoter). It is normal for architects who apply for conditions to pay a small deposit. Time is provided for competitors to study the conditions and ask questions about them. The assessors' answers are circulated to all competitors and a closing date is set for the receipt of designs.

"The conditions can include a cost limit agreed by the promoter. Competitors who exceed the cost limit or break any other mandatory conditions are disqualified.

"All designs are numbered and judged anonymously when referred to the jury of assessors. Designs are judged as soon as possible after the closing date and the promoters and the NZIA are notified of the result in a written report by the assessors. The architect who is declared the winner of the competition is appointed by the promoters to be the architect for the works.

"Competitions in New Zealand normally take one of two forms — for actual building projects, or for ideas where no real building project is involved. They can be conducted in one or two stages."

This outline of the system shows that the professional adviser has more of a supervisory role than in Canada and that the involvement of the assessors and the position of the promoter is closer to the RIBA pattern.

In the New Zealand system, six prizes are scheduled to be competed for, with the author of one of the six designs being selected as the winner who is commissioned for the work and given an advance of 10% of the fees due (based on an estimated project value). If he is not asked to proceed with the work, he is entitled to a further 10%. In a two-stage competition, prizes are awarded at the end of each stage. Equal prize money is awarded to each of six competitors selected to proceed to the second stage and they are each awarded a further sum at the completion of this stage (except for the winner who is given the job on the basis set out above). The promoter has the option to terminate the competition at the end of the first stage on payment of the prize money due. (Assessors' fees and fees payable to the professional adviser are also calculated separately for the first and second stages, unlike the RIBA system where a two-stage competition is really regarded as a single unit and the promoter is still committed to full costs if he decides to abandon it after the first stage.)

The cost of organising a competition is slightly more than in the UK although the system is very similar. (The promoter does, however, have the advantage of the optional second-stage situation.) For instance, the cost to a promoter of a competition for a project valued at $2m is $15,120 (excluding expenses and the winner's fee), compared with RIBA costs of £5,380 on a project valued at £1m. A prizewinner (other than the one placed first) would receive the total prize money of $1,660 (for the two stages) whereas in an RIBA competition of a similar project value, the second-stage participant might receive between £300 and £1,175 (depending on whether he received a major prize or an honorarium).

Entry requirements
The regulations leave the professional adviser to decide upon how much material is to be submitted and how it should be set out. The only guidance given is as follows:

> "*The number and scale and method of finishing the required drawings shall be distinctly set forth. The drawings shall be of the uniform size required by the conditions, mounted on stiff board, drawn clearly to explain the design, so that all the drawings shall be uniform in size, number, mode of colouring, and mounting. As a general rule a scale of 16 feet to an inch will be found sufficient for plans, sections, elevations, or in the case of very large buildings, a smaller scale might suffice, but shall be set out in the conditions by the professional adviser to meet the specific circumstances. (Unless the professional adviser advises that perspective drawings or models are desirable, they shall not be admitted.)*"

The New Zealand Institute of Architects, though not optimistic about the future number of competitions, does claim that there has been an increase in enquiries concerning competitions but fears that a number of clients do not want to get involved with the full procedures set out in the regulations.

Documentation
Australia
Regulations for the Promotion and Conduct of Competitions, issued by the Royal Australian Institute of Architects (revised 1974). Model forms of conditions for:
  Two-stage competitions
  Single-stage and limited competitions
  Ideas competitions
  Chart of competition costs
  Guideline timetables
  Introductory brochure *Architectural Competitions*

New Zealand
Document 1.3.3 *Competition Regulations*, issued by the New Zealand
Institute of Architects (includes the schedule of fees)

Canada
Code for the Conduct of Architectural Competitions, issued by the
Royal Architectural Institute of Canada (revised 1975) (RAIC
Document No. 4)
Guide for Professional Advisers for Architectural Competitions,
issued by the RAIC (RAIC Document No. 5)

13 Competitions in the USA

General attitudes

It is odd that in a country which is known to be so dedicated to competition in so many aspects of its life, architectural competitions should be such rare events. At present there are about five or six competitions a year and most of these are limited, either by invitation or geographically. The years 1974 and 1975 showed a slight increase but, to quote an American Institute of Architects spokesman, "I would not think it necessarily portends a trend." In fact, the AIA seems content to let things stay very much as they are as far as architectural competitions are concerned.

The Code for Architectural Design Competitions, issued by the American Institute of Architects, which governs its members' participation in architectural competitions, was last reprinted in 1972 and included a resolution adopted by the Board of Directors the previous year, authorising the conduct of private limited competitions which allow the sponsor considerably more freedom in their organisation. Although the one competition organised so far under this provision is thought to have been successful, it seems unlikely that this change will mark a dramatic increase in the number of competitions being promoted.

The AIA does not appear to seek to propagate the use of the competition system. In fact, in its preface to the Code for Architectural Design Competitions it states:

"The Institute practically never acts as a sponsor for a competition itself, its role being limited to approving the competition program to insure compliance with the objectives previously stated. It may often prove that the competition method is not the best method for selecting an architect and the sponsor is urged to seriously weigh the advantages and disadvantages."

And again in advising on the organisation of a competition, the AIA documents state:

"Design competitions disrupt ordinary office routine. Important work in progress should not be sacrificed for a speculative opportunity."

With such a lack of enthusiasm shown by the representative body of architectural opinion it is hardly surprising that promoters are not eager to put projects out to competition and that the number of competitions promoted has fallen over recent years.

Government initiatives: the federal architecture project

Other bodies are looking into what competitions have to offer and it is from a government-sponsored study of federal architecture that any initiatives which are taken will arise. In May 1972, as part of a programme to improve all aspects of federal design, President Nixon directed the National Endowment for the Arts (a government-sponsored organisation responsible for design standards)

"to appoint a special ad hoc task force committee to review and expand the publication Guiding Principles for Federal Architecture".

A task force was set up with an advisory committee of agency designers representing twenty different federal agencies, and a report *Federal Architecture : a Framework for Debate*, was produced, which set out measures that might be taken to improve the quality of design.

"Each federal building dollar should be regarded as an investment in a better man-made environment for the nation."

This report, issued as an interim report to stimulate further discussion, discussed at some length the possibility of more extensive use of the competition system:

"For some building types another device for injecting quality considerations into architect selection is the formal design competition, widely used in Europe but less so here, and rarely for contemporary federal buildings."
"Architectural opinion of their value is mixed and it has seemed to the profession in this country a laborious and costly procedure. Established architects are often opposed to competitions, preferring to be evaluated on the body of their work rather than on a single study-and-sketch exercise."

"However, competitions can be especially useful in uncovering fresh architectural talent, and a survey of eighteen competitions held in the US since 1960 showed they had generated a considerable amount of public and professional enthusiasm."

This interim discussion report led to a decision to produce three supplementary reports, going further into particular issues raised. These reports were to deal with "mixed use buildings", "adaptive use of historic structures" and "design competitions". The first two of these reports have now been issued, but the third, though prepared, still awaits publication. It looks at the use of the competition system in the US and abroad, analyses the criticisms which have been made and sets out the advantages of using the competition system more widely. Strongly in favour of more extensive promotion of architectural competitions, the report sets out a programme of action to achieve this.

In the meantime, further research is being undertaken by the National Endowment for the Arts, which has sent a representative to Europe to find out at firsthand how competitions are organised in countries where the record has been one of success. A project which the National Endowment is hoping to undertake is the sponsoring and organising of one or two prototype competitions for projects of varying size and scope. The intention would be to offer to cover the costs and administration of these competitions on behalf of an organisation or company which was willing to put a design out to competition. The National Endowment would then be in a firm position to advise on the organisation of competitions and draw up guidelines.

If the US government can be convinced of the constructive part competitions can play in the federal design programme, moves to promote the system there could mark a turning point for competitions generally. With a federal building programme of some billion dollars a year on the construction of new buildings alone, even a small percentage of competition work would make a significant impact and success here might well influence governments of other countries. This, however, is very much a long-term prospect. As RIBA experience shows, intentions can take a long time to materialise into competitions.

The competition record
The number of competitions held in the USA in the last decade has varied between six and seventeen with a marked trend towards fewer

competitions since 1967. During the years 1961 to 1972 (records for these particular years happen to be available) there were 115 competitions, of which only 22 were open national ones. Of the remainder, 18 were limited by invitation and 59 by region, with 3 competitions for urban renewal and 13 ideas competitions (though with the latter two categories, approval was not always sought from the AIA, so the figures are not accurate). Some of the competitions which have been held are:

Pan American Health Organisation	1961
Boston City Hall	1962
Boston Architectural Centre	1964
University Arts Centre, California	1965
Law School, Washington University	1965
Birmingham-Jefferson Centre	1967
Osaka Pavilion	1967
School of Architecture, Ball State University	1967
Yale Mathematics Building	1969
Chicago Public Library	1970
Redesign of the Mall (Washington, DC)	1971
New Haven Arts Centre	1973
Old age housing, New York	1973
Johns Manville World HQ, Denver, Colorado	1973

As in the UK, project competitions have not always resulted in a building.

Ideas competitions have been kept going for students by the National Institute for Architectural Education, which, as well as sponsoring an annual international competition (The William Van Alen Memorial Award) for students and young architects, organises a number of competitions and prizes within the United States. Several American industries have also sponsored student competitions but the concept of ideas competitions open to the whole profession as in the British system is not widely used.

Competition system
The American competition system, like that of Canada, relies on the services of professional advisers — architects, appointed by the promoter, who undertake to draw up the brief and organise the whole competition on the promoter's behalf.

Types of competition
The term "Design Competitions" is used for all architectural competitions, and they can be in two classes:
Class A: Leading to the erection of a definite project on a definite site.
Class B: Not directly leading to the erection of a definite project on a definite site but providing studies of value and interest to the public and the profession.
The situation is also provided for where the sponsor of a design competition may have a definite project and site but he may not be able to guarantee the construction or provide a definite contract for architectural services. In this case it would be considered a Class A competition, with an appropriate prize to be provided in lieu of the commission.
Competitions may be organised in one or two stages, according to the size and complexity of the project.

Work of the professional adviser
No competition may be organised without the aid of a professional adviser, who must be a registered architect. His duties are to advise those holding a competition as to its form and terms, to write the program, to advise on the choice of competitors (in a limited competition), to answer their questions and to conduct the competition so that all competitors will receive uniform treatment. Once an architect accepts this appointment, he may not subsequently accept a commission as designing or supervising architect for that project, whatever the outcome of the competition. (A similar embargo is laid on the assessors in the UK system.)

Work of the assessors
One point on which the American Institute of Architects competition regulations differ from those of most other institutes is on the link between the work of drawing up the conditions and judging the entries. Most competition systems reinforce this link, asking that those concerned in the judging take part in the preparation of the conditions. In fact, in international competitions this is obligatory, as it is in the RIBA system. However, the AIA Competition Code states that:

"Because the professional adviser has written the program and may therefore be inclined to favor one particular solution of the problem he shall not be a voting member of the jury although he may be present at its deliberations. Likewise members of the jury should

107

not be those who had a part in drafting the program as they may have preconceived opinions and prevent an unbiased judgement based on the problem as set forth in the program."

Jury members are, therefore, appointed solely to judge the designs. The jury may contain lay members but architect members must be in the majority.

Commitment to the winning architect and other prizewinners
In Class A competitions the promoter is required to undertake to appoint the winning architect as architect for the work, and the model form of program which the promoter is asked to follow states:

"The contract will be automatically closed when the envelope containing the name of the winner is opened."

The model form also contains a proviso that if, in the opinion of the owner (i.e. promoter), the winner is lacking in experience, the owner may require him to associate himself with another architect, selected by the winner and acceptable to the owner. The UK system has a similar proviso but places the responsibility for making this decision on the assessors, not the owner. If the architect is not appointed then he is paid a "prize", the amount of which is stated in the program.

In an open competition the winning architect is either awarded a prize or commissioned for the job, as stated above, and other competitors may receive second, third, fourth, fifth prizes, etc. (the number of such prizes is to be stated in the program). The amount of prize money offered has to be agreed with the professional adviser and must be "adequate"

"so that a reasonable number of premiated designs shall receive remuneration at least sufficient to cover the cost of submitting the drawings."

(There does not appear to be a recommended scale.)
Where architects are specifically invited to compete, they must each be paid a fee

"equivalent to the amount normally paid to an architect for the preliminary work involved as though each were the only one submitting work".

The fee paid to the architect selected by the jury as the winner is the only one which can be merged on appointment of the architect to proceed with the work. (This makes AIA limited competitions considerably more expensive than those organised by the RIBA, or indeed by most other organisations, where an honorarium rather than a full fee is paid to each competitor.)

Entry requirements
The notes of guidance (printed in the Code of Design Competitions) to professional advisers state:

> *"Judgement must be based on scheme and not on presentation. If a simple presentation is called for, there will be more time left for the development of the scheme. The professional adviser should remember that if a simple presentation is required it should be made mandatory. Only drawings absolutely necessary to the explanation of the scheme should be required."*

The notes go on to give detailed guidance on the scale and type of drawings which should be requested and, if these recommendations are followed by professional advisers, a competitions program will impose very strict limitations on what competitors may submit and how they may present it. Surprisingly, there seems to be no provision for the use of dyelines or photographically reproduced submissions:

> *"Drawings should be on paper mounted on stiff cardboard and a standard size should be required of all competitors ... In a large competition some of the less important or repetitious drawings may be in pencil on tracing paper mounted."*

And another nicely precise instruction is:

> *"There should be no human or vehicular accessories on any drawing, except that one human figure 5'8" high may be placed on each elevation and section."*

However, no particular method is obligatory and, so long as the institute's requirements of simplicity of presentation and equality of submitted material are followed, the professional adviser is free to set his own standards.

Cost

It is the duty of the professional adviser to see that the promoter's requirements fall within the cost limit allowed, and he is advised:

"The importance of establishing a reasonable estimate cannot be overestimated. If the winner of the competition later gets estimates and finds the established price too low, the onus falls on him and not the professional adviser, who has by then severed his connection with the operation."

No advice is given to the jury on the matter of cost. Although the profession of quantity surveyors does not exist in the USA, architects or engineers specialising in the costing of buildings could presumably be brought in to advise at the final stage. •

Documentation
Code for Architectural Design Competitions, issued by the American Institute of Architects

14 For and against: the competition debate

It would be naive to try to present the competition system as without its critics. Competitions have been described as "an anachronism", "a hangover from the Victorian age", "time-wasting", "risky", "expensive" and "based on a complete misunderstanding of how the architect works" — but they continue, not only in the UK but throughout the world, and the buildings they produce continue to be discussed and visited. Sydney Opera House probably epitomises the competition debate in the eyes of many people as they argue whether it is a masterpiece worth any price or an expensive white elephant. But this really misses the point. The debate is not about the production of national monuments of a higher standard (though there is no reason why this should not be one of the results), but about the quality of design, which can be as apparent in a group of low-cost houses as in an important government building, and how such quality can be stimulated and encouraged in the general practice of architecture.

In countries where the competition system is one of the standard methods of distributing work, schools, housing, churches, banks, civic buildings, sports halls, community centres and health clinics — in fact the buildings which go to make up the fabric of the surrounding environment in any town — have all been designed by this method. No one would claim that every competition produces a masterpiece but the success rate is high. (In the Baden-Würtemberg area of Germany, a survey of 400 promoters found that 92.6% claimed that their expectations had been well fulfilled, 85.5% believed that they had definitely got a better building by going out to competition and 90.7% said that they would use the system again.) It is generally agreed that in those countries where competitions play an important part in the working life of architects, the average standard of design is high. What is not so readily agreed is that this has anything to do with the competition system or, if it has, that competitions would have the effect of raising standards elsewhere.

What are the grounds for doubting the value of the competition system? Prejudice, ignorance, self-preservation and the fear of an open situation can play a part, however hidden, as anyone who has seriously tried to open up a debate on the merits of competitions will testify. These attitudes are, however, changing and what militates most against the competition system at the moment are the very real problems caused by too few competitions, which means that neither architects, promoters nor the general public have enough experience of the system or skill in its use to take full advantage of what it has to offer. The last time there were as many as twenty competitions in any one year in the UK was in 1938. Since then the system has not really been given the opportunity to prove either its strengths or its weaknesses.

The architect/client relationship
One of the most powerfully argued criticisms of the competition system is that it divorces the client from his architect at the most crucial stage of a design — when the concept is being developed. This view is put forward by Derek Senior in his book *Your Architect* (Hodder), written in association with the Royal Institute of British Architects in 1964. His views on competitions, as set out in the book, were those held by many of the profession at the time:

> *"By far the greatest [defect] is that the client has to instruct one architect and appoint another. The winning scheme is designed without direct contact between its author and his client. The mutual stimulation of architect and client on which the achievement of really good architecture must depend has to take place by proxy until the design has got to the sketch stage. The really sensible client, therefore, will use a competition as a means of choosing a designer rather than a design."*

The value of the close architect/client relationship, or dialogue, presupposes the existence of two distinct personalities: the architect, who will be responsible for planning and drawing up the design, and the client, who will build, finance and use the building. However, more and more projects are being designed, not for the user, but for a committee of people with mixed criteria of judgement (economic, social, aesthetic, functional), and the emphasis laid on any particular aspect can change with the relative strength of the representatives of that particular interest. In some cases competitions (particularly the new Regional competitions) have brought the various representatives of the client body face to face with the architects who might design the scheme (and indeed with each other) for the first time and allowed them to see at firsthand how their particular sectional interests interact to affect the design of the building.

The dialogue necessary to develop a design does exist in competitions in the broadest sense and at many different levels. It starts within the promoter's organisation, amongst the people who will be responsible for building the scheme, those who will manage it and those who will live, work or spend their time in it. This establishes the brief. The dialogue continues with the assessors, experts and laymen, who examine the brief together, questioning the presuppositions on which it is based and extending and refining its requirements. The dialogue is then taken up by the competitors, who have the chance to question the promoter either through the written question and answer system or, more directly, through the forum meeting. The individual competitors form groups with colleagues from other professions, spreading the dialogue still more broadly, so that what used to be a one-to-one conversation between the designer and would-be user becomes an open seminar for all who want to be concerned. A dialogue conducted in this way allows architects full range of exploration, without constraints, of all possibilities. At the final meeting of the assessors, the field is narrowed in accordance with the promoter's requirements, and the winning design selected. The client and architect can then meet on a face-to-face basis to develop the design to working drawings with the added advantage that everybody concerned, in the architect's office or in the client body, will by now be fully conversant with each other's aims and requirements.

How is the promoter's timetable affected?
The process of organising a competition is claimed to be too time-consuming for the average promoter seriously to consider finding an architect by this method. In fact, competitions need take no longer than the normal commissioning process (for a small Regional competition), and even in an open two-stage competition (which would take about fifteen months to organise from the finalisation of the brief to the appointment of the winner on the basis of a costed design) the extra time can be accommodated with proper planning. In an article in *Architectural Competitions News,* Eric Lyons writes:

"I have heard that one of the objections to architectural competitions is the time factor — the extra time that is involved in running a competition as compared with 'everyday' methods of selecting an architect. Of course it is true up to a point and in certain circumstances, but where the promoting body has a rolling programme of

work planned for many years ahead, and when one examines the time scale that most projects are subjected to, say in the case of local authorities with their compulsory purchase process, public hearings and so on, it looks fairly obvious that the so-called extra time for a competition is easily absorbed and is of little significance. If we relate this background to the current situation of economic gloom, cut-back of building programmes and general uncertainty, we can see that there is one thing which will not be in short supply, and that is time. Few building promoters can truly say they haven't the time to run a competition."

This point is also taken up in the RIBA's handout explaining the competition system, under the heading "Delays are ruled out":

"Promoting a competition obviously takes time but it must be remembered that the outcome is a real design — chosen as the best —which is based on a careful brief. Once the timetable for a competition is fixed it imposes a discipline on all concerned and ensures that the necessary decisions are made clearly and on time."

People tend to be optimistic as far as time is concerned, under-estimating how long they spend visiting buildings, getting decisions made and readjusting schedules in the normal design process. It is difficult to make a direct comparison but competitions do not have a bad record where the promoter is really determined to get ahead. To take the Paris Arts Centre as an example, work started on the site within a year of the announcement of the result and continues to progress fast.

Do the winners have the experience to carry out the job?
Competitions, it is argued, attract young architects and, however brilliant their design capabilities, what a promoter needs is an experienced team with the knowledge to carry the job through.

Competitions do tend to be won by young architects (but not because only young architects enter: if you look at recent UK competitions you will find some established firms amongst the second-stage also rans). It is also true that an outstanding design is not all a promoter wants from an architect, but it is a very good starting point. As an American commenter put it:

"An 'inexperienced' architect with the ability to win a competition is a public resource deserving to be nurtured."

114

Most competition rules recognise the potential difficulties and safeguard the position of the promoter either by allowing him to select a scheme other than the one chosen by the assessors as the winner or by requiring a young architect to associate himself with a more experienced team to carry out the project. In public authorities in Germany, the winning team sometimes moves into the promoter's own architectural office, working as a design unit within the larger organisation for the development period of the competition. In the UK, assessors are asked to satisfy themselves that the winning architect has the resources to carry out the work and to report, in confidence, to the RIBA on their findings. The new Promoter Choice competition also allows a promoter to interview the architects of a number of schemes, selected through an open competition, before appointing any one of them as architect for the work.

But young architects can handle a large commission successfully and have done so frequently in the past. They know that this is the work on which their future will depend and they give it a special type of dedication which the promoter would not get in the ordinary run of things. It can also be argued that the very inexperience of young architects leads them to demand high standards which older people would have learnt not to expect, and to fight for the integrity of a design where compromise would be an easier solution.

The costs of competitions and the buildings they produce
Another argument against competitions is that of the extra cost involved. One local councillor in the UK vetoed a proposal to hold a competition for a housing scheme after she had worked out that it would add nearly £100 to the cost of every dwelling.

In fact, an RIBA competition adds about .5% to 2% to the cost of a project (though not if a promoter uses the Regional Special Category competitions where his costs are virtually nothing). If you compare the cost of promoting a competition with that of commissioning more than one design in the normal way, in the RIBA system the break-even point is reached before the promoter is able to commission even two schemes to competition design stage. Competitions do cost money to promote, though set against other building costs, the extra is not very great. Whether it is worth it depends on the outcome.

Competition buildings are said to be more expensive and people who hold this view can point to a housing competition which has come in over yardstick or to a scheme which had to be abandoned for lack of money. Non-competition schemes also suffer from this trouble. What the promoter does have in the competition situation is considerably more control over the cost, if he chooses to implement his rights in this respect. In most systems, including that of the RIBA, where cost is an important factor, the promoter can state a cost limit, based on current prices, in the conditions. The promoter's representative can be delegated to pay special attention to this factor and a quantity surveyor (selected and appointed by the promoter) can, and usually does, go through the final shortlist of designs to check that they can be built within the set limit (updated, of course, to take account of inflation). If properly used, these are considerable safeguards.

In Germany, the competition system is recommended to promoters as a way of saving money, if that is what is important to them. Competition winning designs, they claim, can be selected on the basis of a more economical plan and good design always pays in the long term.

Architects' architecture

With a system designed to place the choice of winner in the hands of the architect-dominated jury of assessors some people believe that the result will be "architectural" rather than what the promoter and the general public want. This is not basically a criticism of the competition system but more an indictment of the state of architecture in the UK and elsewhere, if standards of excellence and quality within the profession are at such odds with those of everybody else. There has been one well publicised case of a lay/architect split on a competition jury, but it is much more usual for the laymen and the professionals to work harmoniously together, each side appreciating what the other has to offer, and coming to understand each others' points of view more fully as the competition progresses.

What can happen at the present time when there are so few competitions is that assessors (architects and lay) feel that they have to pick an "out of the ordinary" design to justify the process. (In practice, they do not often give way to this temptation.) A competition winner needs to be in no way extraordinary except in the quality of its design.

Public participation

Competitions attract attention. Too few competitions may attract too much attention, focusing so much interest on the one result that those concerned with its implementation cannot make any move without being scrutinised. This is not a criticism of the competition system but a sign of the potential interest in the built environment, which is given no other outlet.

The general attitude towards architects and what they produce is not an encouraging one. Very little is done to excite interest or encourage the appreciation of even the best modern buildings. Known buildings disappear to be replaced by new schemes but nobody bothers to explain why the building is there, why it has taken that particular form or what special purpose it has been designed to serve. It is hardly surprising, therefore, that the attitude of the general public is to cling on to existing buildings which they can appreciate and understand. A competition opens up the whole design and building process. The brief is published and discussed, so the intention to build is known to everyone. The results are covered by the press and media, the schemes are exhibited and public meetings are often held to explain the design.

This wider involvement in the discussion of what constitutes good design is one of the most positive contributions the competition system has to make, not only to the architectural profession but to society. A greater interest in what is being built in our cities, towns and villages, can only lead to better standards of design. It is very much needed.

Appendix A
Definition of terms

Assessors

The assessors are the people appointed by the promoter to conduct a competition. In the UK, their duties include advising the promoter on the brief, drawing up the conditions, answering questions, selecting the winning designs and reporting on these designs and the response to the competition to the promoter. There are between three and seven assessors on a jury (an odd number is recommended unless the chairman is given the casting vote), and the majority are architects. They are normally nominated by the promoter and approved by the president of the institute responsible for approving competitions (i.e. the RIBA in the UK). The jury may also include lay assessors, nominated by the promoter to represent his interests. In most competition systems the assessors are responsible for the whole organisation of the competition and the decisions taken, but in those countries where a professional adviser is appointed, the assessors' only duty is to judge the designs. (See *Professional Adviser* below.)

Assessors' report

This is a confidential statement from the assessors to the promoter about the competition and the quality of the designs. In most cases it may be made public, but only if the promoter so wishes.

Award

The award of the assessors is the official statement of their decision, setting out the allocation of prizes, honoraria and special mentions.

Brief

The brief is the statement of the promoter's requirements and forms one part of the competition conditions.

Code

In the UK, and as far as RIBA members are concerned, the word 'Code' refers to the RIBA Code of Professional Conduct. The competition regulations issued by the American Institute of Architects

119

and by the Royal Architectural Institute of Canada are also called a Code but, in this book, the word is used in this sense only in Chapters 12 and 13 (on competitions in the Commonwealth and the USA).

Conditions

The conditions (called the program in the USA and in Canada) set out the basis of the competition. They are drawn up by either the assessors or the professional adviser and before being issued to competitors, they must receive the approval of the organisation responsible for regulating competitions in the particular country concerned. A full set of competition documents making up the conditions may include the brief, instructions on submitting entries, site plans and photographs, entry form and official envelope. Once the question and answer document (in some cases referred to as an explanatory memorandum) has been issued it forms part of the official conditions and these are legally binding on the promoter.

Deposit

The deposit is the sum of money which has to be paid by a competitor before he can receive the conditions. It is not required in all competitions. Where required, it is returnable, unless otherwise stated, to anyone declining to compete and returning the documents by a given date as well as to those submitting bona fide entries.

Honorarium

This is a term used in RIBA competitions (and in some others based on the RIBA model) to describe the set amount of money which is to be given to all competitors in a limited competition or in the second stage of a two-stage competition. It is paid to those competitors who do not receive one of the main prizes. In other systems, such as the AIA system, it is just referred to as a fee.

Jury

The jury is the group of people responsible for selecting the winning design and judging the entries. It normally comprises only the assessors but may include the professional adviser. In some cases there may be two juries, one professional and one lay.

Model Forms

Some institutes issue model forms of conditions to supplement their competition regulations. These set out the basic clauses of the conditions, providing a "model" for the promoter.

Official Envelope
In order to preserve anonymity, competitors are often issued with a standard envelope in which to seal their entry forms. The sealed envelope is sent with the entry and identified with a number by the promoter. It is not opened until after the assessors have made their decision and reported it to the promoter.

Premiums
The premiums are the prizes awarded to the winning designs in the RIBA system. In project competitions there are usually three prizes awarded in order of merit. In ideas competitions and in Developer/ Architect competitions there may be one first prize and an additional sum to be allocated at the assessors' discretion. The prizewinning designs may be referred to as premiated designs.

Professional Adviser
In some countries (for instance the USA, Canada and Switzerland) an architect is appointed to organise the competition on behalf of the promoter. He is often responsible for writing the brief and drawing up the conditions and takes over much of the work and responsibility of the assessors in other systems.

Program
See *Conditions.*

Promoter
The promoter is the individual or organisation who issues the invitation to architects or students (or occasionally the general public) to submit designs in accordance with his brief which is set out in the conditions. He may also be referred to as the client, or in the case of project competitions, as the owner. In the USA and Canada he is called the sponsor.

Purchases
In international competitions and in some European competition systems, a certain amount of money is set aside to "purchase" interesting designs which have not been given major prizes. This is normally a way of awarding additional prize money and does not necessarily mean that the copyright has been bought.

Registration
This is the process by which a competitor confirms his intention to

submit a design. Not all competitions require competitors to register but it is normal practice in international competitions.

Regulations
Regulations for the promotion and conduct of architectural competitions are issued by the national organisations responsible for regulating competitions in their own countries or by the International Union of Architects (UIA) for international competitions. In the USA and Canada the word "Code" is used for these regulations.

Report
Competitors are often permitted to submit an explanatory report (usually strictly limited in length) to accompany their designs.

Supervisor
In the RIBA system an architect is appointed to advise the promoter in the early stages of a competition. Once the assessors are appointed his work is finished.

Technical Examiners
Assessors may ask the promoter to appoint technical examiners to check the details of the submissions and to see whether the designs fulfil the requirements of the brief. Such examiners, who are usually architects, are called upon only to report to the assessors, in accordance with instructions, and do not have any right to reject a scheme.

Appendix B: RIBA regulations for the promotion and conduct of competitions

Introduction

1. These Regulations have been drawn up to ensure that architectural competitions are properly conducted and that the selection of designs shall be on merit alone and shall satisfy a promoter's requirements. The RIBA Code of Professional Conduct does not allow architects to give unpaid services in competition with each other except through competitions organised within the framework of these Regulations.

Outline of procedure

2. Competition assessors are appointed; their function is to prepare the instructions to competitors. Invitations are issued by the promoter and competitors apply for particulars. Designs are submitted anonymously and the assessors award the premiums and report to the promoter, who undertakes to accept the decision and to appoint the winner as architect for the work.

Types of competition

3 Competitions may be grouped broadly as follows:

a 1. Competitions for an actual building project conducted in a single stage. In these, fairly complete small scale drawings, plans, sections, elevations etc. sufficient to explain the scheme are required.

2. Competitions for an actual building project conducted in two stages. In the first stage only planning on a broad basis is required with simple line drawings on a small scale sufficient to indicate the intentions of the competitor. From first stage competitors a small number, say from 6 to 10, will be selected to proceed to the second stage in which the work required will be as for a single stage competition — paragraph (*a1*) above.

3. Competitions for an actual building project conducted in two stages. The first stage is open as in (*a2*) above; the second stage consists of the competitors selected from the first stage together with a limited number of competitors specifically invited to submit schemes at the second stage. Persons invited to submit entries at the second stage shall be named in the conditions.

b Competitions of ideas set as an exercise to elucidate certain aspects of architectural and planning problems. The winner of such a competition is not subsequently commissioned to carry out a building from the competition design. These competitions are normally open to all architects and frequently to students of architecture also. The promotion of an ideas competition purely for advertising purposes or restricted to the use of some proprietary product is not acceptable.

Entry to the competitions described in paragraph (*a*) above may be either open, or limited by invitation or selection, or restricted by locality, and is confined to architects as defined in Regulation 18.

Assessors
4 *a* Since the success of a competition will depend largely upon the experience and ability of the assessors, these appointments require the greatest care. There should not be more than one lay assessor to two architect assessors. It is unusual for a single assessor to be appointed but if such is the case, for example in the case of competitions having a project value of less than £200,000 he must be an architect who is free to recommend that other assessors be appointed to act with him. The names of the assessors must appear in the competition conditions and in any advertisement relating to the competition.

b The President of RIBA in consultation with the promoters will nominate assessors for appointment by the promoters. Assessors should, in the main, be architects of acknowledged standing but may also include a layman or laymen, which will allow promoters to participate closely in competitions and will enable them to contribute their specialised knowledge to the preparation of the competition brief.

c 1. If the intending promoter is a local or other authority the promoter shall decide whether or not its employees shall be permitted to enter the competition.
2. If employees are permitted to compete and the promoting authority desires that its Borough or its County Architect etc. shall be an assessor he must be one of a jury consisting of not less than three architect assessors.
3. Such additional architect assessors shall not be employees of the promoting authority.
4. The promotion authority may not appoint more than one of its members or non-architect officers to act as the lay assessor.

124

5. If the promoting authority has permitted its employees to enter the competition and the Borough or County Architect etc. has been appointed as an assessor the technical examiners appointed under Regulation 11 shall not be employees of the promoting authority.

5 Where an architect already holds the appointment of consultant to the promoters, and it is the intention that he should act as consultant to the architect appointed as a result of a competition, it must be so stated in the conditions and he must not act as sole assessor, but may be one of the jury of assessors on which there is more than one architect member. With this exception and subject to the provisions of Regulation 4(c) no architect appointed as assessor for a competition may thereafter act in any capacity as architect, joint architect or consultant for the work nor may any member of the promoting body nor any partner, associate or employee of the promoting body or of the assessor do so, nor may he or they compete or assist a competitor in the competition.

6 In the event of being invited to act after the conditions of a competition have been drawn up, assessors must, before consenting, confirm that the conditions are in accordance with these Regulations, and have been approved by the RIBA.

Duties of assessors
7 The jury of assessors should appoint one of their number as chairman. The duties of the assessors are as follows:

a To take the promoter's instructions and ascertain his requirements. The assessors should undertake any investigation or research that may be necessary to produce the programme, setting out the promoter's requirements in the form of clear and detailed instructions to the competitors.

b To advise the promoter on the type of competition to be held, the time to be allowed for submission of designs and the premiums which should be offered.

c To draw up the competition conditions in consultation with the RIBA Competition Supervisor (Regulation 43), and to convey in detail the promoter's requirements to competitors in the form of instructions for their guidance, which must incorporate the clauses of these Regulations applicable to the particular competition. In this connection, special care must be taken to state clearly which conditions and instructions are binding to the extent that disregard thereof would involve disqualification, and which are for guidance only.

d To answer questions submitted to the promoter within a limited time by competitors and to advise the promoter as to the method and form of sending out answers. In a two-stage competition it is open to assessors to issue a further statement to guide competitors in the final stage.

e To examine all the designs submitted by competitors; to determine whether they conform to the binding conditions and instructions and to exclude those which do not.

f To make their Award in strict accordance with the conditions. The Award should be in the form of a formal statement signed by all the assessors setting out the number of designs examined and the order of the premiums awarded. The Award should be accompanied by a separate report to the promoter informing him of the quality of the designs submitted, of the merits of the premiated and commended schemes and other schemes of interest and, where necessary, of any modifications which ought to be made to the winning scheme.

g To convey to the Secretary RIBA and to the Competition Supervisor a copy of their Award and Report at the same time as it is conveyed to the promoter.

h To settle any dispute that may arise between the promoter and the winner as to the terms of his appointment by the promoter as architect for the project, before the signing of the contract of appointment. The assessors' duties are completed when the successful competitor is appointed as architect in accordance with Regulation 31 or, in the case of an ideas competition, when the premiums are paid.

Assessors' fees
8 The scale of charges for architect assessors is as follows:

a Where there is a jury of two or more architect assessors, each assessor shall receive a personal fee equal to 20% of the value of the first premium; where there is a single architect assessor, as in the case of competitions having a project value of less than £200,000, his

126

personal fee shall be 40% of the value of the first premium.

b In the case of ideas competitions a minimum personal fee of 100 guineas is payable to each assessor and thereafter agreed in negotiation with the RIBA.

9 The above fees are exclusive of travelling and out-of-pocket expenses which may be charged in addition by each assessor.

10 Lay assessors' fees are a matter for negotiation between the lay assessor and the promoters.

Technical examiners
11 The assessor/s shall be free to appoint technical examiners to assist in the preliminary stages of the judging of the competition. Such technical examiners shall be architects and subject to Regulation 4(*c5*) may be assistants in the assessor's/s' own practice or department, who by virtue of Regulation 5 are not eligible for the competition. Payment for technical examiners shall be on a time basis in accordance with the RIBA Conditions of Engagement and shall be payable by the promoters to the employer who makes the technical examiners' services available.

12 The appointment of technical examiners shall in no way reduce the responsibility of the assessor/s to the promoters. The technical examiners shall be bound to secrecy and shall not be present during the judging otherwise than in accordance with paragraph (*c*) below. The technical examiners shall not be empowered to exclude any submitted designs and their duties shall include the following:

a To examine projects, to check (against a pro forma provided by the assessor/s) that the mandatory aspects of the conditions have been met;

b To note on a check list any documents submitted but not required by the conditions. It shall be the duty of the assessor/s to decide whether any such document shall be eliminated before adjudication of the designs;

c To be present if required during the adjudication to answer any factual questions put to them by the asssessor/s concerning any of the projects.

127

Premiums and honoraria

13 No fewer than three premiums should be offered. In a competition other than an ideas competition, the first of these premiums represents a payment on account of fees payable to the winner when engaged as architect to carry out the project. Discretion should however be given to assessors to aggregate the second, third and other premiums and divide the total amongst a larger number of competitors if the circumstances merit it. Where such discretion is exercised, assessors must still indicate an order of merit in a competition for a building project against the eventuality provided for in Regulation 25. The amount of the premiums should be related to the estimated cost of the project and in accordance with the RIBA schedule of premiums and honoraria.

14 In the case of a two-stage competition for a building project, each second stage participant must receive either a premium or an honorarium in accordance with the RIBA schedule of premiums and honoraria. These are awarded at the conclusion of the second stage.

15 In a limited competition for a building project, each competitor must receive either a premium or an honorarium in accordance with the RIBA schedule of premiums and honoraria.

Invitations

16 The promoter's invitation to architects to compete must state clearly the nature of the project, the limits of cost where these are applicable, the name/s of the assessor/s, the latest date for applying for competition conditions, the definition of those eligible for entry, the amount of the deposit required, the latest date for submission of questions, the latest time and date for the submission of designs, and the premiums offered. Invitation notices should be published in the monthly and weekly technical journals and a copy should be sent for publication in the *RIBA Journal*.

17 Where a deposit is required, it must be returnable to the competitor immediately after the publication of the assessor's/s' award or, in the event of an applicant declining to compete, on his returning to the promoter his copy of the conditions and all annexed documents no less than four weeks before the closing date for the submission of designs.

18 The word 'architect' means any person who, at the time of his application for the competition conditions and of submission of the competition entry is registered under the Architects' (Registration) Acts, 1931 and 1938, or being qualified for registration, has already made application to the Architects' Registration Council in the prescribed form to be admitted to the Register. Any applicant for the conditions must state his registration number, and in the case of an unregistered person who has made application for registration, the date of such application and the number of the receipt issued by the Architects' Registration Council in respect of the admission fee. Where application is made by a firm, the registration number or numbers of the architect partner or partners of the firm must be given. In this context a firm is defined as a partnership properly established for the purpose of architectural practice, or an association for the purpose of entering the current competition: in the latter case there must be in existence a partnership agreement for the purpose of carrying out the project in the event of the association winning the competition.

19 Regular teaching staff and present students of a school of architecture are precluded from participating in a competition in which a member of the staff is acting as sole assessor but not in a competition where there is more than one assessor of whom one only is a member of the staff.

Competition documents

20 The promoter must issue to each competitor a printed copy of the conditions of the competition prepared by the assessors in conformity with the RIBA Model Form of Conditions together with a site plan showing ground levels, positions of services and all relevant information. Before such conditions are issued, a private promoter must sign one copy of the conditions over a sixpenny stamp: conditions issued by a corporate body may have to bear the common seal of that body, the appropriate stamp duty becoming payable. The requirement of sealing does not apply in Scotland or other countries where the law on sealing of contracts is different.

Competitors' questions

21 Competitors should normally be permitted to ask questions designed to clarify the instructions. Such questions must be sent in by a stated date, after which an explanatory memorandum based on the

questions submitted must be circulated quickly to all competitors, which then forms part of the instructions for the competition; this should clarify but not alter or modify the published conditions. Depending on the nature and size of the competition, a minimum period of 4 weeks from the date of publication of the competition conditions should be allowed for the submission of the questions. The preparation of a general statement answering the questions should take no longer than the stated period allowed for the submission of questions. If unforeseen delays occur, a compensating extension of the final date for the submission of designs should automatically be made and notified at the beginning of the statement.

Drawings and report required
22 The number, scale and method of finishing the required drawings must be distinctly set forth. The drawings must not be more in number or to a larger scale than necessary clearly to explain the design, and such drawings should be uniform in size, number and mode of presentation. The drawings must be accompanied by a concise typewritten report describing the buildings, explaining their construction, finish and materials proposed to be used, and giving such information as cannot be clearly shown on the drawings. Where required the report should include an estimate of the cost, based upon any recognised method of calculation which may be directed by the assessor/s. In a two-stage competition, the drawings submitted in the first stage should be the minimum required to indicate the principles of the competitor's design and may be supplemented by a written statement outlining the competitor's objectives.

In appropriate circumstances, the assessor/s may permit or require the submission (specifically limited in scope) of:

a perspective drawings or axonometric drawings in line form (or similar diagrams to indicate three-dimensional organisation of a design), or

b block models or photographs of block models, where appropriate, or

c explanatory diagrams in competitors' reports.

For two-stage competitions this material should be restricted to the second stage. In all cases the preparation of elaborate drawings or presentation material is to be avoided.

Method of submitting designs

23 No design may bear any motto or distinguishing mark of any kind but each design must be accompanied by a declaration by the competitor contained in an official envelope issued by the promoter with the instructions. The declaration must state that the design is the competitor's or joint competitors' own personal work, and that the drawings have been prepared in his or their own offices, and under his or their own supervision, and that he or they undertake/s to accept the assessor's/s' award. Each design and envelope on receipt must be given a serial number by the promoter but the envelope must not be opened until after the assessor's/s' award has been made.

Disqualification

24 A design shall be excluded from the competition for any of the following reasons:

a If received after the latest time stated in the conditions.

b If, in the opinion of the assessors, it does not give substantially the accommodation asked for.

c If it exceeds the limits of site as shown on the plan issued by the promoter, the figured dimensions on which shall be adhered to.

d Subject to Regulation 39 if the competitor's estimate exceeds the cost limit stated in the instructions or if the assessors shall determine that the probable cost will exceed such cost limit.

e If any of the conditions or instructions, other than those of a suggestive character, are disregarded.

f If a competitor shall disclose his identity or improperly attempt to influence the decision.

Award

25 It is the duty of the assessors to make an award, and the promoter and competitors must undertake to accept that award. Each assessor must bind himself to accept the jury's Award even where this is on the basis of a majority decision. The promoter must undertake to pay the premiums and honoraria accordingly and to appoint the author of the design placed first as architect for the work, unless the assessors shall be satisfied that there is some objection valid under these regulations to such appointment, in which case the author of the design placed second in order of merit shall be appointed, subject to a similar condition, and so on. It may also be desirable that some designs of merit which did not receive premiums should be commended. In selecting such designs, the assessors must be guided by the same considerations as in awarding premiums.

26 If in exceptional cases the assessors anticipate difficulty in making an award they should refer the matter to the President of the RIBA for guidance.

27 The promoter must notify all competitors of the result of the competition before any public announcement is made.

Exhibition of designs
28 In the case of single-stage competitions all accepted designs and accompanying reports together with a copy of the assessors' Award must be publicly exhibited for not less than six days. Notice of the time and place of exhibition must be given to all competitors and to the public. Nevertheless, where large numbers of entries have been received, selected numbers may be exhibited in relays for periods of six days, provided that the premiated and commended designs are exhibited throughout the whole period. In the case of two-stage competitions, first-stage designs may also be exhibited at the end of the competition at the discretion of the promoters.

Copyright
29 The ownership of copyright in the work of all competitors will be in accordance with the Copyright Act 1956.

Return of drawings
30 All drawings submitted except the design selected for execution must be returned carriage paid to the competitors within fourteen days of the close of the exhibition.

Appointment of the architect
31 Subject to the provisions of Regulation 25, the promoter must formally appoint the author of the design selected for execution as architect for the work. A standard form of contract of appointment for this purpose is published by the RIBA. Any dispute as to the terms

of the appointment before the signing of the contract shall be settled by the assessor acting, if necessary, as arbitrator between the promoter and the winner. The standard form of contract of appointment provides for any subsequent dispute between promoter and architect to be referred to an independent arbitrator nominated by the President or a Vice-President for the time being of the RIBA.

32 The author of the selected design may be required to satisfy the assessors that he has the resources to carry out the work efficiently. If they are not satisfied that he possesses or can develop a suitable organisation they may, at their discretion, after consultation with the author of the selected design advise the promoter that a second architect should be appointed to collaborate with the author of the selected design in carrying out the work, but without obligation on the promoters to pay any additional fees. The assessors will be prepared if necessary to assist the author of the selected design and the second architect in agreeing a suitable apportionment of the fees which could otherwise be due to the former.

Architect's fees
33 The appointed architect shall be paid in accordance with the applicable scale of professional charges sanctioned and published by the RIBA, the competition premium which he received being deemed to be a payment on account towards the total fees payable.

34 If as a result of a competition other than a competition of ideas or a limited competition, the promoter fails to make a formal appointment under Regulation 31 or if after appointment no instructions are given to the appointed architect within two years of the date of the award, he shall be paid an additional fee of the same amount as the premium originally paid to him as author of the design placed first.

35 In the event of the promoters deciding to proceed with part only of the work the appointed architect shall be paid whichever shall be the greater of either the scale of fees in accordance with Regulation 33, or an amount ascertained by aggregating the additional fee payable under Regulation 34, with the original premium paid.

36 If, however, no instructions are given to the competitor selected for the appointment as architect as a result of a limited competition within two years of the date of the award, he shall be paid one and a

half per cent on the estimated value of the work provided that where the architect's fees are based on the application of the RIBA scale of professional charges to repetitive housing works he shall be paid one-quarter of the total fee which would become payable if the work were to proceed to completion. The premium originally paid will merge in these fees.

37 In the event of the promoter subsequently instructing the appointed architect to complete the entire project the original premium paid and any other fees paid under Regulations 34, 35 and 36 shall merge in the full-scale fees for such entire project.

Conditions of engagement
38 The employment and the carrying out of the work shall be in accordance with the RIBA Conditions of Engagement unless varied by agreement under Regulation 31.

39 Where between the date of the issue of the competition conditions and the date of the award increases have occurred in the costs of labour and materials, the effect of such increases shall not prejudice the design or estimate of the appointed architect as the cost limit shall be adjusted to take account of such increases.

Modifications
40 The appointed architect may be required to modify his design to meet any reasonable requirements of the promoter within the original brief without the payment of any extra fee, and the cost limit shall be adjusted to suit such modifications. The appointed architect shall be entitled to additional fees in accordance with the RIBA Conditions of Engagement in respect of additional work resulting from any change in the promoter's brief.

41 If when tenders are received the lowest tender exceeds the appointed architect's competition estimate or the cost limit stated in the instructions as either or both may be varied under Regulation 39, the appointed architect shall be given the opportunity of submitting further proposals to achieve a reduction of the tender price, provided that such proposals do not radically alter the appointed architect's original design upon which tenders were invited. Any work incurred by the appointed architect in preparing and submitting such revised proposals shall not entitle the appointed architect to any additional fee but no part of the competition premium shall be repayable to the

promoter even if the finally modified tender price exceeds the cost limit originally stated or as varied under Regulation 39.

RIBA supervisory charge

42 In order to assist with the provision of adequate supervision and advice a charge of 20% of the value of the first premium in all competitions shall be paid by the promoter to the RIBA when the competition conditions have been approved by the RIBA and before they are issued to participants.

43 Detailed guidance in the conduct of competitions shall be provided by the RIBA Secretariat and a competition supervisor appointed from the RIBA panel of competition supervisors. Such a supervisor shall be appointed to each competition to approve the draft conditions prior to their publication and to be available to advise the assessors and the promoters at all stages of the competition.

Power of waiver

44 The President of the Royal Institute shall have the power to waive or to vary any of these Regulations in circumstances where in his view the best interest of the client or the profession would justify that course.

Amendments to the 1968 revision

Since the major revision of the Regulations for the Promotion and Conduct of Competitions in 1968, a number of amendments have been agreed by the Council of the RIBA. One is to allow students, with the agreement of the promoter, to enter the first stage of a two-stage competition provided that they undertake to form an association with a Registered Architect if selected to proceed to the second stage. The second change gives the President the right to nominate at least one-third of the architects invited to enter a limited competition and the compensation fee (see Regulation 34) has been brought in line with that payable in other competitions.

The Competitions Working Group has also agreed to amend the Regulation which allows local authority employees to enter a competition promoted by that authority to make it clear that this does not apply to the Chief Officers (ie Borough Architect, etc.) who must remain ineligible. Regulations 3, 4, 18 and 34 are, therefore, amended as follows:

Types of competition
3 The last paragraph now reads 'Entry to the competitions described in paragraph (a) above may be either open, or limited by invitation or selection, or restricted by locality and is confined to architects as defined in Regulation 18. Where a number of architects are specifically invited or selected by the promoter the President of the RIBA shall have the right to nominate at his discretion at least one-third of those invited or selected to compete.'

Assessors
4 *Section c* Amended to read 'If the intending promoter is a local or other authority the promoter shall decide whether or not its employees shall be permitted to enter the competition. In no case shall the Chief Architect or other Chief Officers of the authority be permitted to enter the competition.'

Eligibility to compete
18 This Regulation is now sub-divided into (a) and (b) with part (a) as original regulation:

'(b) With the agreement of the promoter, students of architecture may submit entries in the first stage of two-stage competitions on the condition that, if a student competitor is selected to proceed to the second stage, he forms an association with a Registered Architect for the purpose of completing the competition. The words 'students of architecture', for the purposes of competitions to which this clause refers, means students who, at the time of application for conditions, are student members of the RIBA or have applied for membership thereof.'

Architect's fees
If, as a result of a competition other than a competition of ideas, the promoter fails to make a formal appointment under Regulation 31 or if, after appointment, no instructions are given to the appointed architect within two years of the date of the award, he shall be paid an additional fee of the same amount as the premium originally paid to him as author of the design placed first.

Appendix C: Regulations for international competitions in architecture and town planning issued by UIA

Introduction

The purpose of these Regulations is to state the principles upon which international competitions are based and which must be observed by a promoter in drawing up the conditions for a competition. They have been drawn up in the interests of both promoters and competitors.

General provisions

Article 1 The designation "international" shall apply to any competition in which participation is open to architects or teams of technicians led by architects of more than one country and members of other professions working in association with them. Competitions in which no restriction of any kind is placed are termed "open". These Regulations cover both *open* and sometimes *special* competitions where some form of restriction is imposed. The different types of competition are set out in the Instructions and Recommendations to Promoters.

Article 2 International competitions may be classified into "Project" or "Ideas" competitions or a combination of the two.

Article 3 International competitions may be organised in One or Two stages.

Article 4 The conditions, including the programme of requirements of an international competition shall be identical for all competitors.

Article 5 A copy of the complete competition conditions shall be filed with the International Union of Architects and sent free of charge at the same time to all UIA National Sections. The anwers to competitors' questions shall also be sent to the UIA and to all UIA National Sections.

Article 6 Competition conditions which are not published in one of the official languages of the International Union of Architects (English, French, Spanish and Russian) shall be accompanied by a translation into at least one of these languages. Such translations shall be issued at the same time as the original language version. Competitors shall not be required to submit material in more than one UIA language.

137

Article 7 All competitors' designs shall be submitted anonymously.

Article 8 Notice of an international competition shall be issued by the promoter and/or the UIA Secretariat General to all National Sections with a request for publication in technical journals or through other media at their disposal, as far as possible simultaneously, to enable those interested to apply for the competition conditions in due time. This announcement shall state where and how the competition documents may be obtained and that the conditions have received UIA approval. (See Article 15.)

Professional adviser

Article 9 The promoter will appoint a Professional Adviser, preferably an architect, but who could be a town planner in the case of a planning competition, to prepare the conditions and supervise the conduct of the competition.

Drawing up the conditions

Article 10 The conditions for international competitions, whether single or two stage, open or restricted, shall state clearly: (a) the purpose of the competition and the intentions of the promoter, (b) the nature of the problem to be solved, (c) all the practical requirements to be met by competitors.

Article 11 A clear indication shall be made between the mandatory requirements of the conditions and those which permit the competitor freedom of interpretation, which should be as wide as possible. All competition entries shall be submitted in a manner to be prescribed in the conditions.

Article 12 The information supplied to competitors (social, economic, technical, geographical and topographical) must be specific and not open to misinterpretation. Supplementary information and instructions approved by the jury may be issued by the promoter to all competitors selected to proceed to the second stage of a two-stage competition.

Article 13 The competition conditions shall state the number, nature, scale and dimensions of the documents, plans or models required and the terms of acceptance of such documents or models. Where an estimate of cost is required, this must be presented in standard form as set out in the conditions.

Article 14 As a general rule, the promoter of an international competition shall use the metric scale. Where this is not done the metric equivalent shall be annexed to the conditions.

UIA approval

Article 15 UIA written approval of the draft competition conditions, including the time-table, registration fee and membership of the jury shall have been received in writing by the promoter before any announcement is made by the promoter that a competition has received UIA sponsorship.

Registration of competitors

Article 16 As soon as they have received details of the competition, competitors shall register with the promoter. Registration implies acceptance of the competition conditions.

Article 17 The promoter shall issue to competitors all the necessary documentation for preparing their designs. Where a deposit is required for the competition conditions, unless otherwise stated this deposit shall be returned to competitors who submit a bona fide design.

Article 18 The names of those competitors selected to proceed to the second stage of a two-stage competition will only be made public at the discretion of the promoter and the jury in which case they will be published in alphabetical order.

Prizes, honoraria and mentions

Article 19 The competition conditions must state the amount and number of prizes. The prizes awarded must be related to the size of the project, the amount of work involved and the expense incurred by competitors.

Article 20 Town planning competitions are, by their nature, Ideas competitions, since the work is generally carried out by official bodies, frequently on a long-term basis. It is therefore particularly important for the promoter to allot adequate prize money to recompense competitors for their work. It may even be the sole remuneration received by the first prize winner.

Article 21 The promoter undertakes to accept the decisions and the award of the jury and to pay the prizes allotted within one month of the announcement of the competition results.

Article 22 Each participant in a competition by invitation shall receive an honorarium in addition to the prizes awarded.

Article 23 In two-stage competitions, a reasonable honorarium shall be paid to each of the competitors selected to take part in the second stage. This sum, which is intended to reimburse them for the additional work carried out in the second stage, shall be stated in the competition conditions and shall be in addition to the prizes awarded.

Article 24 The competition conditions shall state the use to which the promoter will put the winning scheme. Plans may not be put to any other use or altered in any way except by agreement with the author.

Article 25 In Project competitions the award of first prize to a design places the promoter under an obligation to entrust the author of the design with the commission for the project. If the winner is unable to satisfy the jury of his ability to carry out the work, the jury may require him to collaborate with another architect of his choice approved by the jury and the promoter.

Article 26 In Project competitions provision shall be made in the competition conditions for the first prize winner to receive compensation of a further sum equal to the amount of the first prize if no contract has been signed within twelve months of the announcement of the jury's award. In so compensating the first prize winner the promoter does not acquire the right to carry out the project except with the collaboration of its author.

Article 27 In Ideas competitions, the promoter, if he intends to make use of all or part of the winning scheme, will, wherever possible, consider some form of collaboration with its author. The terms of collaboration must be acceptable to the winner.

Insurance
Article 28 The promoter will insure competitors' designs from the time when he assumes responsibility for them and for the duration of his responsibility. The amount of such insurance will be stated in the competition conditions.

Copyright and right of ownership
Article 29 The author of any design shall retain the copyright of his work; no alterations may be made without his formal consent.

Article 30 The design awarded first prize can only be used by the promoter upon his commissioning the author to carry out the project. No other design, whether premiated or not, may be used wholly or in part by the promoter except by agreement with the author.

Article 31 As a general rule, the promoter's right of ownership on a design covers one execution only. However, the competition conditions may provide for repetitive work and specify the terms thereof.

Article 32 In all cases, unless otherwise stated in the conditions, the author of any design shall retain the right of reproduction.

The Jury

Article 33 The jury shall be set up before the opening of the competition. Their names and those of the reserve members of the jury shall be stated in the competition conditions.

Article 34 As a general rule the members of the jury are appointed by the promoter after approval by the UIA. The UIA will assist promoters in the selection of jury members.

Article 35 The jury shall be composed of the smallest reasonable number of persons of different nationality, and in any event should be an odd number and should not exceed seven. The majority of them shall be architects.

Article 36 It is required that one member of the jury should be appointed by the UIA and this should be stated in the competition conditions.

Article 37 There should not be more than two representatives of the promoting body included in the jury.

Article 38 It is essential that all members of the jury be present at all meetings of the jury.

Article 39 Each member of the jury shall see and approve the competition conditions before they are made available to competitors.

Article 40 No member of the jury for a competition shall take part, either directly or indirectly, in that competition, nor be entrusted either directly or indirectly with a commission connected with the carrying out of the object of the competition.

Article 41 No member of the promoting body nor any associate or employee nor any person who has been concerned with the preparation or organisation of the competition shall be eligible to compete or assist a competitor.

Article 42 The decisions of the jury shall be taken by a majority vote, with a separate vote on each design submitted. In the event of the vote being split, the Chairman shall have the casting vote. The list of awards including the jury's report to the promoter shall be signed by all members of the jury before they disperse and one copy of this document sent to the Union.

Article 43 In two-stage competitions, the same jury should judge both stages of the competition. In no case may a competition which has received UIA approval as a single stage competition proceed to a second stage except with UIA approval of the conditions and with appropriate remuneration to the competitors involved over and above the premiums provided for in the original competition. In the event of such a secondary competition taking place, the jury appointed in the original competition must be reappointed.

Article 44 Any drawings, photographs, models or other documents not required by the competition conditions shall be excluded by the jury before examining a competitor's entry.

Article 45 The jury may disqualify any design which does not conform to any of the conditions, instructions or requirements of the competition.

Article 46 The jury must make an award. The award shall be final and shall be made public.

Article 47 The fees and travel subsistence expenses of jury members shall be paid by the promoter.

Exhibition of entries

Article 48 All designs, including those disqualified by the jury, shall be exhibited for at least two weeks together with a copy of the signed report of the jury. The exhibition shall be open to the public free of charge.

Article 49 The promoter shall notify registered competitors in all countries in good time of the date and place of the public exhibition of designs. He shall similarly inform the UIA and all National Sections. Photographs of the premiated designs shall be sent to the UIA with a view to possible publication.

Article 50 In two-stage competitions, designs submitted in the first stage shall be kept secret until the final results are announced.

Return of designs

Article 51 All drawings and plans, other than those which have received an award and are retained by the promoter will be destroyed at the end of the public exhibition, unless provision is made to the contrary in the competition conditions. Where models are required, these will be returned to their author at the expense of the promoter within one month of the close of the public exhibition.

Instructions and recommendations to promoters

1.1 Project and Ideas competitions

International competitions may be either "Project" or "Ideas" competitions or in certain circumstances a combination of both. The aim of a Project competition is to find the best solution for an actual building project and to appoint its author to carry out the commission. Competitions of Ideas are set as an exercise to elucidate certain aspects of architectural and planning problems. The winner of such a competition is not commissioned to carry out the project, and hence students of architecture may participate at the discretion of the promoter.

1.2 *Classification of competitions*

Class A — Open competitions

Competitions in which professionals from all countries may participate without restrictions of any kind are termed "Open".

Class B — Limited competitions

Class B1 — Regional competitions

Competitions which are limited to professionals of two or more countries having common cultural, historical and/or professional links are termed "Regional", and may be organised on the basis of national regulations which have received the prior approval of the UIA. A list of such regulations is filed with the UIA Secretariat General. Where the promoting country has no competition rules of its own, a regional competition may be held on the basis of the UIA Regulations or the national regulations of a country which have received the prior approval of the UIA.

Class B2 — National competitions with invitations to foreigners

In certain circumstances the promoter of a national competition open to all or certain architects from one country may wish to invite a limited number of architects from other countries to participate. In this case, national regulations apply with the proviso that the number of architects from countries other than the promoting country may not exceed three and that the jury includes at least one architect member and one reserve from a country other than the promoting country. Each invited participant must receive an honorarium.

Class B3 — Competitions by invitation

Where a promoter wishes to invite a number of named architects from two or more countries to submit designs in competitions, such a competition may be organised on the basis of the national regulations of the promoting country, where these exist and have the prior approval of the UIA, or on the basis of the UIA Regulations. Each participant invited must receive an honorarium.

Class C — Special competitions

A promoter may wish to invite participation in a competition other than those described under Classes A and B, for example, competitions combining town planning as well as design problems, competitions involving the use of industrialised components, or competitions involving the participation of developers. In these and other circumstances the promoter may wish to limit participation to professionals or groups of professionals having certain expertise or experience. In such cases, the field of expertise must be clearly defined in the preliminary information issued by the promoter. Competitions proposed in this class should be referred to the UIA at the earliest possible opportunity to permit adequate consultation between the UIA and the promoter.

1.3 *Competition organisation*
International competitions may be organised either in one or two stages.

1.3.i *Single-stage competitions*
In competitions conducted in a single stage fairly complete small scale drawings, plans, sections, elevations, etc., sufficient to explain the scheme are required. Such competitions are recommended for small projects only, that is to say up to an estimated value of US$1 million.

1.3.ii *Two-stage competitions*
The first stage is a competition of ideas and therefore only planning on a broad basis is required with simple line drawings on a small scale sufficient to indicate the intentions of the competitor. From the designs submitted in the first stage the jury selects a small number, for example, 10; the authors of these designs are invited to take part in the second stage, but their names are not released until the final award has been made at the end of the second stage. However, all competitors are informed whether or not they have been invited to take part in the second stage. In order to maintain anonymity, it is the responsibility of the Professional Adviser, or similar functionary not connected with the jury, to open the envelopes containing the names of the authors of the designs retained for the second stage. The envelopes are then resealed until the final award has been made.

If necessary, after the end of the first stage, the jury may, with the agreement of the promoter, clarify or amplify points in the competition conditions for the benefit of second stage competitors. Such additional instructions may not disclose in any way the solutions proposed by any of the first stage competitors. Only in exceptional circumstances may the time interval between the judging of the first stage designs and the delivery of second stage designs exceed six months. In such circumstances the promoter must inform the UIA of the reasons for the delay and of the measures it is proposed to take in consequence.

The second stage of a two-stage competition may, if necessary, be limited to part only of the subjects dealt with in the first stage. The same jury will be required to judge both stages and to award the prizes. The publication and exhibition of all designs submitted, including first-stage designs, will take place after the final award has been made. Publication of any design retained for the second stage before the final award has been made will entail disqualification.

Students of architecture may be allowed to participate in two-stage competitions on the understanding that, if they are selected to go forward to the second stage, they do so in association with a qualified architect.

Two-stage competitions are recommended for town planning and large-scale projects, that is to say, over an estimated value of US$1 million.

2 *The promoter*

2.1 The promoter may be an individual, a corporate body or a number of corporate bodies who have come together by agreement for the purpose of sponsoring a competition. The promoter or all the promoting bodies involved must undertake to accept the decisions and award of the jury and to pay the prizes allotted within one month of the announcement of the competition results.

3 *Professional adviser*

3.1 A Professional Adviser, preferably an architect, should be appointed and paid by the promoter and his appointment approved by the UIA Secretary General. His role is to supervise the conduct of the competition and the preparation of the conditions. His functions include ensuring that the competition timetable is adhered to, supervising the receipt of competitors' questions, the despatch of the jury's reply to all competitors and the receipt of competition entries, and safeguarding the anonymity of competitors at all times. He will assist the jury and will be present during its deliberations but he will have no vote. His responsibilities will be limited to those involving the organisation of the competition.

4 *Competition conditions*

4.1 The careful preparation of the competition conditions including the schedule of requirements is of primary importance to the success of a competition and therefore adequate time should be allowed for this phase of the competition.

4.2 It is stressed that the publication of the conditions constitutes the offer of a contract by the promoter. In registering for the competition, the competitor accepts this contract. The competition conditions together with any reply to competitors' questions constitute the legal basis for this contract, which is legally binding on both promoter and competitors. Promoters are therefore urged to use the Model Forms of Conditions which the UIA has drawn up as a basis for all competitions submitted for its approval.

4.3 The draft conditions of competitions held under the auspices of the UIA must be submitted to the Union for approval before publication and issue to competitors (exceptions may be made in the case of competitions in Classes A and B where the UIA by devolution has given its prior approval to national competition regulations and where a copy of the conditions has been filed with the UIA at the same time as they are issued to competitors). The UIA may at its discretion approve other types of competition (Class C).

4.4 The members of the jury should, where practicable, be consulted in the preparation of the conditions and schedule of requirements. In any event, each member of the jury must formally approve the conditions before these are published and issued to competitors.

4.5 It may be desirable to indicate to competitors in the conditions the promoter's priorities in regard to a solution to the problem (for example, functional aspects, economy in construction or in use, solution to technical or circulation problems, etc.).

4.6 It is emphasised that the number of documents (drawings, etc.) required from competitors should be kept to the minimum necessary for the jury to understand and evaluate the designs submitted.

5 *The jury*

5.1 There is considerable advantage in restricting the number of jury members. Where possible these should not exceed seven and it is desirable that there should be an odd number of members.

5.2 The jury shall be composed of a majority of architects, or in certain cases, of architects and other qualified professions, such as town planners or engineers. The majority of members of the jury should be composed of professionals who are foreign to, and who live and practise, outside the promoter's country. The jury should be selected for their particular knowledge of the subject of the competition.

5.3 Reserve members of the jury should be appointed in the proportion of one reserve to four members of the jury including the UIA representative. Reserves should attend meetings of the jury, without the right to vote, in order to replace a full member in the event of his death or unavoidable absence, even during the judging.

5.4 At its first meeting the jury shall elect a Chairman from among its members.

5.5 The jury may recommend the appointment by the promoter of technical consultants to help them in their work.

6 *Anonymity*

6.1 It is essential that the anonymity of competitors should be maintained until the final judgment and in the interests of the competition system rigorous measures should be taken to ensure that this principle is adhered to and is seen to be adhered to.

6.2 The Model Forms stipulate that each competitor should place a six-digit stencilled number 1 cm high on all plans and accompanying documents which constitute his entry. This number is recorded by the Professional Adviser on the register of competitors and the identity of the competitor remains confidential until after the award of the jury and the signing of the jury's report to the promoter.

6.3 There are various methods of maintaining anonymity in the despatch of competitors' designs. One method is to use the name of the promoter as the sender, and to quote the promoter's name on both the receipt for despatch and on the covering letter to the promoter enclosing the receipt. All these documents would bear the competitor's code number. The only key to the competitor's identity is then contained in the special envelope containing his name and address which is enclosed with his entry.

7 *Competition timetable*

7.1 The time limits set by a promoter for the different phases of an international competition are frequently too tight, and this frequently leads to an extension of time being granted. This can be avoided by early consultation with the UIA and by reference to the Guidance Notes for Promoters.

7.2 Sufficient time must be allowed between the distribution of the competition conditions and the closing date for registration by competitors and similarly for the receipt of questions submitted by competitors, taking into account transport delays. The members of the jury must also be given adequate time in which to consider their replies.

7.3 The final date and time for the despatch of entries by post or other means, including delivery by hand, must be specified in the competition conditions, as well as the final date and time for their receipt by the promoter (see Model Forms). Sufficient time must be allowed for transport: this may be between three and six weeks in the case of an open competition involving competitors from throughout the world. In the case of late arrival of any entry, it is the responsibility of the jury to decide whether the entry was despatched in accordance with the competition conditions and whether circumstances permit its admission to the judging.

7.4 The competition timetable may under no circumstances be shortened.

7.5 The judging dates, which should be agreed at an early stage with the members of the jury, should be published in the competition timetable which forms part of the conditions issued to competitors. In the case of a two-stage competition, it may only be possible to announce the dates of the judging of first stage entries. The judging dates should take into account the time required for despatch of designs, customs clearance and the hanging or other arrangement of designs for the judging. Experience has shown that a week is generally sufficient for judging an average competition.

7.6 Any unavoidable delays in the judging must be agreed by the jury and must be publicly announced.

8 *Customs*

8.1 Experience has shown that customs clearance of competition entries may take longer than anticipated. The promoter should therefore make prior arrangements with the customs authorities to ensure speedy clearance of projects. If, however, having taken all reasonable precautions the promoter does not receive a competitor's entry by the last date for receipt stated in the conditions, the promoter cannot be held responsible.

9 *Cost estimates*

9.1 In an international competition it is often difficult to give a sound basis for a cost estimate. However, competitors may be asked to provide information on the floor area (m^2) or volume (m^3) of the building for the purpose of comparison by the jury.

9.2 It is also possible to appoint independent consultants to compare the costs of certain projects which have reached the last stage of selection, and before the final judgment is made.

9.3 It is recommended that the cost estimate should not be a determining factor in the jury's decision, except where cost limits are imposed in the competition conditions.

10 *Distribution of prize money*

10.1 The total sum allocated for prize money must be stated in the competition conditions. It is usual for the jury to award a first, second and third prize, but the prize money may be otherwise allocated at their discretion.

10.2 It is customary for the promoter to set aside a global sum for mentions and sometimes also for the purchase of schemes which have particular merit, and to be awarded at the discretion of the jury. This must be clearly stated in the conditions and any decision not to award the total amount of the prize money allotted by the promoter must be taken unanimously by the jury.

10.3 In some countries the Tax Authorities deduct a certain percentage of the monies awarded to prize winning competitors. Where this applies the promoter must ensure that a statement to this effect appears in the competition conditions, so that foreign architects competing are aware that the prize money quoted is subject to deduction.

11 Pre-examiners

11.1 Pre-examiners are appointed by the promoter (their number to be determined according to the number of designs submitted) to check that designs fulfil the mandatory requirements of the competition conditions. This task is carried out on the basis of a pro forma approved by the jury.

11.2 Pre-examiners will take no part in the judging process nor will they be permitted to eliminate any design. They may only report to the jury any deviations from the programme.

12 Presentation of projects to the jury

12.1 The promoter is required to place a Secretariat at the disposal of the jury to minute their meetings, record their decisions and provide such interpretation and translation as may be necessary.

12.2 All competition designs must be presented to the jury and judged in identical conditions. It is recommended that premises of adequate size should be provided for judging the designs submitted to avoid handling as far as possible. Where handling of projects is required during the judging, staff should be available to do so. The jury should also have a conference room at their disposal.

13 Exhibition of entries

13.1 All designs, including those disqualified by the jury together with the names of their authors are in principle exhibited for at least two weeks together with a copy of the signed report of the jury.

13.2 Competitors have the right to remain anonymous if their designs are not premiated or purchased by so indicating on the envelope containing their declaration/proof of identity form. In this case they forfeit their registration fee.

14 *Appointment of the architect*

14.1 If for reasons of distance it is impracticable for the winner to carry out the project from his country of residence, the jury may recommend that he enters into partnership with an architect of the promoting country.

14.2 If the winner is unable to satisfy the jury of his ability to carry out the project, the jury may require him to collaborate with an architect of his choice and approved by the jury and the promoter.

14.3 The appointed architect may be required to modify his design to meet any reasonable requirements of the promoter within the original brief.

15 *Settlement of disputes*

15.1 Since no Regulations, however well drawn up, can preclude all possibility of disputes, provisions for conciliation and arbitration must be included in the competition conditions.

15.2 The jury members are the sole arbiters at all stages up to the final award of prizes.

15.3 In the event of a dispute not related to the judging process or the award of prizes, the matter will be settled by an arbitration process approved by the UIA and without recourse to the legal authorities of the promoting country.

15.4 The arbitration body could be the UIA College of Delegates or in exceptional cases the Bureau, or any other qualified body of recognised impartiality.

15.5 Another arbitration procedure could be the appointment of three arbitrators, one to be nominated by each party and the third by mutual consent of the first two. Where mutual agreement cannot be reached on the choice of the third arbitrator he could be nominated by the UIA College of Delegates or the Bureau.

15.6 The expenses resulting from any conciliation or arbitration procedure is to be shared between the parties concerned.

16 *Cost of organising an international competition*

16.1 It is impossible to predict the exact cost of an international competition, and promoters are therefore advised to contact the UIA Secretary General at an early stage and he will give advice in the light of the type of competition suitable for the project. Costs may also vary in different parts of the world and according to the facilities available to the promoter.

16.2 *Prizes*: the value of prizes to be awarded in an international competition varies according to the size and complexity of the project.

As a general guide, the total prize money should be in the region of 0.6% of the estimated cost of the building. For very small projects (e.g. US $250,000) the total prize money should be approximately 1% of the estimated building cost, whereas for very large projects (e.g. $10,000,000) prize money might be about 0.4% of the estimated building cost.

16.3 *Consultants' fees*: it may be necessary to commission consultants for the preparation of the conditions and the checking of competition entries, in certain cases from overseas. Their fees may range between US $2,500 and US $5,000 (January 1973 rate).

16.4 *Fees for jury members*: each foreign member of the jury should receive approximately US $300 per day, the exact amount to be determined by the promoter taking into account the circumstances of the competition. Fees should never be less than US $175 per day (January 1973 rate). The same rates apply to reserve members of the jury. Jury members' travel and subsistence expenses will also be met by the promoter.

16.5 *UIA fee*: the promoter will undertake to pay the UIA a non-reimbursable fee of US $600. (This is normally payable when the file is opened by the Secretary General.) In addition, the promoter will pay the UIA 5% of the total value of the prize money when the competition is launched, that is to say when competitors are invited to apply for the competition conditions. This latter sum is reimbursable if the competition does not proceed.

16.6 *Other costs*:

16.6.i Possible travel and subsistence expenses of consultants

16.6.ii Survey of the site

16.6.iii Publicity for the competition

16.6.iv Printing of the competition conditions including site plans, photographs, etc.

16.6.v Arrangements for receiving entries

16.6.vi Fees and expenses of the professional adviser and pre-examiners

16.6.vii Hire of premises if necessary for the judging of competition entries and the public exhibition of projects

16.6.viii Insurance of competition projects while in the possession of the promoter

16.6.ix Return of entries (usually models only)

16.6.x Publication of the competition results

16.6.xi Secretariat expenses (interpretation, translation, correspondence, etc.).

NOTES

NOTES

NOTES

NOTES